Family-Based Treatment for Restrictive Eating Disorders

Family-Based Treatment for Restrictive Eating Disorders unpacks some of the most common dilemmas providers face in implementation of family-based treatment (FBT) across the spectrum of restrictive eating disorders. Directed toward advanced clinicians and supervisors, this manual is rooted in the assumption that true fidelity requires ongoing self-reflection and an understanding of the nuances involved in translating manualized interventions into rich clinical practice. Combining the key tenets of FBT with the best practices in supervision, it provides a framework to support each phase of the treatment process. Each chapter contains a wealth of resources, including clinical vignettes, a treatment fidelity measure and other useful tools to assist both supervisors and advanced clinicians in becoming expert FBT practitioners.

Sarah Forsberg, PsyD, is a psychologist in the Department of Child Psychiatry at the University of California, San Francisco, where she conducts training and research in the eating disorders program. She began her pursuit of research and clinical interests in the treatment of childhood eating disorders in 2005, and has since been involved in numerous clinical trials involving family based treatment pursue research and clinical interests in the treatment of childhood eating disorders. Her focus is on treatment development, as well as the dissemination and training practices surrounding family-based treatment for eating disorders.

James Lock, MD, PhD, is a professor of child psychiatry and pediatrics and associate chair in the Department of Psychiatry and Behavioral Sciences at Stanford University School of Medicine, where he also serves as director of the eating disorder program for children and adolescents. Dr. Lock has published over 300 articles, abstracts, books and book chapters. He has been continuously funded by the National Institutes of Health since 1998. His recent research focuses on integrating treatment research with neuroscience in eating disorders, including examining neurocognitive processes and their functional and neuroanatomical correlates. He has lectured widely in the US, Canada, Europe, South America, Asia, Australia and New Zealand. He was awarded the Price Family Foundation Award for Research Excellence in 2010, and the Leadership Award from the International Academy of Eating Disorders in 2014.

Daniel Le Grange, PhD, is Benioff UCSF Professor in Children's Health and eating disorders director in the Department of Psychiatry and the UCSF Weill Institute for Neurosciences at the University of California, San Francisco. He also is emeritus professor of psychiatry and behavioral neuroscience at the University of Chicago. Dr. Le Grange has been funded by the National Institutes of Health and others to support his work in psychosocial treatment development for adolescents with eating disorders. He has presented his research in North America, Europe, South Africa, Asia and Australia. He is a recipient of the 2013 UCSF Presidential Chair Award as well as the 2014 Leadership in Research Award from the International Academy of Eating Disorders.

Kathleen Kara Fitzpatrick, PhD, is a psychologist and Director of the Outpatient Eating Disorder Clinic in the Department of Child and Adolescent Psychiatry and Behavioral Sciences at Stanford and Stanford Children's Hospital. She has expertise in family-based therapeutic approaches and translational neuroscience-based treatments for children, adolescents and young adults with eating disorders. She is interested in therapeutic innovation and treatment development.

Family-Based Treatment for Restrictive Eating Disorders
A Guide for Supervision and Advanced Clinical Practice

Sarah Forsberg, PsyD,
James Lock, MD, PhD, &
Daniel Le Grange, PhD

Routledge
Taylor & Francis Group

NEW YORK AND LONDON

First published 2018
by Routledge
711 Third Avenue, New York, NY 10017

and by Routledge
2 Park Square, Milton Park, Abingdon, Oxon, OX14 4RN

Routledge is an imprint of the Taylor & Francis Group, an informa business

© 2018 Taylor & Francis

The right of Sarah Forsberg, James D. Lock and Daniel Le Grange
to be identified as authors of this work has been asserted by them in
accordance with sections 77 and 78 of the Copyright, Designs and
Patents Act 1988.

Library of Congress Cataloging-in-Publication Data
A catalog record for this book has been requested

ISBN: 978-0-8153-6953-0 (hbk)
ISBN: 978-0-8153-6957-8 (pbk)
ISBN: 978-1-351-25202-7 (ebk)

Typeset in Bembo
by Apex CoVantage, LLC

I would like to acknowledge the many incredible supervisors who have shaped and elevated my practice of family-based treatment, including James Lock, Kara Fitzpatrick and Daniel Le Grange. In addition, it is the many patients and families who have taught me about the nuances of FBT and inspired me in their dedication and persistence in the face of many challenges. On a personal note, I wish to thank my own family, who is unwavering in their confidence in me and support of this work. —S.F.

I dedicate this book to the many wonderful students and clinicians I've had the opportunity to mentor and teach at Stanford and around the world. —J.L.

This book is for all the energetic, smart and dedicated mentees I have had the privilege of working with all these many years. —D.L.G.

Brief Table of Contents

Contents

10 Additional Considerations and Future Directions 128

SARAH FORSBERG, JAMES LOCK AND DANIEL LE GRANGE

Acknowledgments

We would like to specifically acknowledge the contributions of the following expert FBT supervisors, consultants and clinicians whose collective wisdom on the practice and supervision of FBT was gathered in a series of interviews for this book: Kathleen Kara Fitzpatrick, Katharine Loeb, Angela Celio Doyle, Renee Rienecke, Andrew Wallis and Kristen Anderson.

1 Orientation to This Manual

Sarah Forsberg, James Lock and Daniel Le Grange

This manual was developed with the aim of facilitating fidelity to family-based treatment (FBT), and is specifically aimed at guiding supervisors and advanced clinicians. This guideline is rooted in the assumption that supervision is a distinct area of professional competence, and that true fidelity requires ongoing self-reflection and an understanding of the nuances involved in translating manualized interventions into rich clinical practice. Over the past decade, the evidence base for FBT has grown significantly, and currently is the recommended first-line approach for treatment of adolescents with anorexia nervosa (AN) (Agras et al., 2014; Le Grange, Lock, Loeb, & Nicholls, 2010; Lock, Agras, Bryson, & Kraemer, 2005). Preliminary evidence suggests it is also preferable to individual cognitive-behavioral therapy for adolescent BN (Le Grange, Lock, Agras, Bryson, & Jo, 2015), and can be useful in treating atypical AN (Hughes, Le Grange, Court, & Sawyer, 2017). There have been significant and successful efforts to disseminate the model outside the academic institutions in which it was developed (Couturier et al., 2014; Hughes et al., 2014). However, a need-service gap remains and access to the treatment is limited given the significant resources required to provide training that assures the highest level of competence in delivery of the model. As a result, efforts to both improve efficiency and decrease cost of training of mental health professionals in FBT are underway.

Background on Treatment Fidelity

Treatment fidelity is a term utilized in psychotherapy research to describe the extent to which an intervention is delivered as intended (Perepletchikova, 2011). It encompasses adherence to prescribed practices, abstention from proscribed interventions, and the sophistication with which the intervention is delivered. Therapists practicing with fidelity are steeped in the core philosophy and principles of an approach, and are able to flexibly apply interventions to meet a unique patient's needs, while remaining adherent. Without fidelitous implementation of an approach it is impossible to evaluate treatment efficacy. Many factors, including lack of training, misunderstanding of the mechanics behind core principles, and a tendency in clinical practice to use integrated approaches, may explain treatment failures. In instances of poor treatment outcome, it is not uncommon for clinicians to attribute lack of progress externally to the family/patient, the treatment or a poor fit between the two. Here, we propose that therapists who are interested in practicing FBT with the highest degree of integrity instead turn to this manual, to expert colleagues and supervisors and to introspection with the aim of refining their skillset in delivering the approach. We hope that this framework will enhance one's confidence and help guide treatment decision making, including decisions about when changing course is indicated.

The Art of Supervision

The practice of clinical supervision is designed to enhance overarching therapeutic skill and promote self-reflection and metacognitive process, and serves an important gatekeeping function in preparing clinicians to practice independently. Historically, supervision has received little attention as a distinct professional entity requiring separate training, and the assumption has been that high levels of clinical proficiency form the basis of quality supervision. This view of "supervision by osmosis" often pervades the field of mental health intervention; however, it has increasingly come under scrutiny given the push for competency-based training. Very few mental health providers receive specific training in supervision and only recently did the American Psychological Association publish its own guidelines for clinical supervision (American Psychological Association, 2015). There are other published guidelines that focus on supervision models that can be applied globally across treatments (i.e., a competency-based approach; Falender & Shafranske, 2014), or specifically within a given model (Milne & Reiser, 2017). However, there is a lack of materials delineating best practices in supervision (Reiser & Milne, 2012). Manuals for therapy promote adherence to treatment protocols; specifically FBT providers referencing the treatment manual had much higher rates of compliance with treatment principles in one survey (Kosmerly, Waller, & Robinson, 2015). Thus the need for a parallel guide for supervisors to prevent drift and enhance adherence is warranted. And yet, there is a significant discrepancy between the strong push for competency-based models of intervention and the lack of coherent training protocols, guidelines and manuals for supervision, even when these are required in RCTs. Attempts to delineate standards for competent supervision have been complicated by diverse viewpoints and difficulties in reaching consensus (Reiser & Milne, 2012).

As a distinct professional activity, supervision involves the provision of education and training to support the development of a high quality of clinical practice. Supervisors not only are responsible for ensuring that their supervisees are competent in the particular therapeutic approach but also guide their professional development. They monitor supervisee adherence to ethical and legal guidelines, as well as their upholding of the values of their respective field of practice. As such, they are leaders and gatekeepers responsible for protecting the well-being of patients, the professional field and society at large (Falender & Shafranske, 2014).

Delineating the Utility of This Manual

There are a few distinctions to be made in considering how this manual is to be applied in clinical practice. First, it is important to distinguish between supervision and consultation. Many involved in dissemination of FBT serve as consultants to licensed mental health providers interested in certification in FBT. The crux of this distinction is that the consultee does not need to accept the directives or advice of the consultant, whereas supervisors are responsible for comprehensive knowledge of the entire case, and are ethically and legally responsible for the patient's welfare. Supervisees operate under their supervisors' professional licenses and thus are required to follow through on directives provided in supervision (whether there is disagreement and how to manage this are separate issues). The manual here provides specific guidance around supervision practices; however, the guidance around structure and helping supervisees walk through common dilemmas will be equally applicable in the consultant-consultee relationship. Those who are qualified to provide supervision in FBT are those who have a specific expertise in the model and aspire to practice with the highest degree of competency. This manual is also directed at assisting such advanced practitioners in enhancing self-reflection and adherence to the model. The foremost purpose of this manual is to enhance fidelity to the FBT model with the aim of improving clinical outcomes.

What This Manual Is Not

This manual is not meant to provide a thorough review of supervision best practices or a review of various models of supervision, or to expand upon universal dilemmas encountered in psychotherapy supervision. We highly encourage supervisors to turn to well-established resources designed to enhance the overarching practice of supervision. We recommend the following guidelines derived from a competency-based perspective of supervision (Falender & Shafranske, 2004) and evidence-based perspective (Milne, 2009).

Best Practices in Supervision

As noted earlier, the APA and others interested in elevating the art of clinical supervision have published guidelines (American Psychological Association, 2015; Falender & Shafranske, 2014; Milne & Dunkerley, 2010). The practice of supervision generally is assumed to include self-assessment (by both supervisee and supervisor), whereby bidirectional feedback is encouraged, and goals with regards to establishing competency and skill acquisition are identified and monitored directly. Different governing bodies have unique requirements one must meet in order to practice. For example, the APA requires minimum training and continuing education for those who wish to practice supervision. Competency in supervision is thought to require a focus on models and theories of supervision, relationship formation, rupture and repair, diversity and multiculturalism, and decision making regarding the developmental level of the supervisee (Bernard & Goodyear, 2014; Falender & Shafranske, 2014, Newman, 2013). Other guidelines exist around remaining sensitive to issues of diversity that arise in the patient-therapist relationship, and supervisor-supervisee relationship. The emphasis is on creating a collaborative environment, whereby expectations are communicated clearly and reviewed on an ongoing basis, and differences with regards to diversity are openly discussed. Supervisors are expected to model professional behavior and thereby socialize individuals into the field (and to "think like" an FBT therapist, in this case). Feedback to supervisees is critical and should be timely and directly linked to FBT competencies. Supervisors create an environment in which therapists feel comfortable providing their own feedback on the supervision process, especially recognizing the tendency for supervisors to overestimate their competence (Walfish, McAlister, O'Donnell, & Lambert, 2012). In this way, supervisors are sensitive to the inherent power differential in the supervisor-supervisee relationship, which is influenced by a range of factors (developmental level, diversity issues, sources of privilege and oppression) (American Psychological Association, 2015). Many of these expectations for the process of supervision can be outlined in a supervision contract to be reviewed with the supervisee when the relationship is established, and supervisors adhere to institutional standards with regards to provision of a contract.

In this manual, we discuss the ways in which supervisors can set the supervisory framework, which includes orientation to required training, methods of evaluation and the structure of supervision.

Who Is This Manual For?

Advanced clinicians practicing FBT have expertise in the treatment of adolescent eating disorders (ED) and have received specialized training in the model, which includes ongoing supervision specifically focused on evaluation of fidelity. FBT supervisors are highly trained experts who have treated numerous families using the approach, and have become supervisors by virtue of their strong theoretical grounding in the model and high-quality clinical work experience. Standards for supervisors have not yet been articulated, but over time will be promulgated. This manual serves as a guide both for those advanced clinicians who seek to elevate their practice of FBT and those who are providing supervision, and reflects competencies that need to be developed for those who are interested in growing into a supervisory role. At a minimum, supervisors are expected to be familiar with the professional standards governing the practice of supervision in their field, and are well versed in the ethical and legal standards of care governing the practice of psychotherapy. Note that the term "clinician" is used throughout to describe any professional treating a family in FBT and also encompasses supervisees.

How to Use This Manual

The structure of this supervision manual generally parallels the structure of the published treatment manual and is divided according to treatment phases: Orientation and assessment, Phase I, with an emphasis on Sessions 1 and 2, as well as middle and ending sessions in this phase. It will focus on common problems that arise during Phases II and III and will address the process of termination (Lock & Le Grange, 2015). Throughout the manual, the parallel process between supervision and treatment is highlighted—for example, as a clinician would work to orient a family to the in-session and overarching structure of treatment, so too does a supervisor take a similar approach to orienting his or her supervisees to the supervision process. The manual therefore highlights the structure and process of supervision, the overarching theoretical model upon which treatment goals are formulated, principles of family engagement, and common supervisor dilemmas that arise reflecting common barriers in provision of treatment. Clinical case vignettes associated with each phase of treatment are integrated throughout to help supervisors and advanced clinicians develop strategies and language to address common challenges in the approach. FBT is a present-focused, solution-oriented model, and so too do supervisors work to address problems clinicians may have in important areas of implementation (e.g., engaging families in the treatment process, understanding family patterns that maintain anorexia nervosa (AN), designing interventions collaboratively with families to promote parental empowerment and understanding and addressing barriers to success). Further, more recent efforts to codify fidelitous delivery of FBT have led to the development of a fidelity-rating tool for Phase I. This measure has been found to be reliable and valid and may support supervision efforts (Forsberg et al., 2015). The measure is included as are suggestions for its use in supervision.

An Important Note About Diagnostic Focus

This manual primarily focuses on the treatment of restrictive eating disorders (R-EDs), including anorexia nervosa (AN), atypical AN and other specified EDs that are restrictive in nature. Many of the dilemmas faced in treatment of R-EDs parallel those faced in FBT for individuals with bulimia nervosa (BN), for example. However, there are also some distinct nuances involved in treating this population that are beyond the scope of this manual. For example, individuals with AN and BN may share similar degrees of body image disturbance, but the focus of addressing this via weight restoration in AN is replaced with an emphasis on disrupting binge/purge episodes and normalizing eating patterns in BN where individuals may alternatively need to maintain weight.

Background Summary

At the beginning of each chapter a summary of the focus of the phase and important background considerations are outlined. In the background section, you will also find information on developmental considerations, to assist you in evaluating the experience level of the trainee and/or exploring your own developmental goals as a clinician.

Common Dilemmas

As you proceed, you will note a review of carefully selected dilemmas the authors chose to review based on their common occurrence in FBT. The challenge will be described and supervisory interventions will be introduced to support resolution of these dilemmas.

Supervisory Tools

Worksheets, guidelines and other resources will be provided throughout, as will case examples to illustrate helpful strategies. These tools may be used to support the structure of the supervision process as well as promote adherence to FBT principles and interventions. For example, we include a fidelity instrument developed for the first phase of treatment. This instrument may serve multiple functions:

- Help therapists prepare and guide them during the session to ensure nothing is left out;
- Help both the supervisor and therapist in supervision to structure the discussion;
- Serve as a guide to monitor progress and allow for self-reflection. For example, you can utilize this to encourage anticipation of challenges based on training background and personal style, problem-solve around common challenges (e.g., the supervisee finds him- or herself attracted to causal discussion, or is uncertain about how to invite siblings to participate in a supportive role), and evaluate progress in learning.

References

Agras, W. S., Lock, J., Brandt, H., Bryson, S. W., Dodge, E., Halmi, K. A., . . . Woodside, B. (2014). Comparison of 2 family therapies for adolescent anorexia nervosa: A randomized parallel trial, *JAMA Psychiatry*, 71(11), 1279–1286.

American Psychological Association. (2015). Guidelines for clinical supervision in health service psychology, *American Psychologist*, 70(1), 33–46.

Bernard, J. M., & Goodyear, R. K. (2014). *Fundamentals of clinical supervision* (5th ed.). Boston: Pearson.

Couturier, J., Kimber, M., Jack, S., Niccols, A., Van Blyderveen, S., & McVey, G. (2014). Using a knowledge transfer framework to identify factors facilitating implementation of family-based treatment. *International Journal of Eating Disorders, 47*(4), 410–417.

Falender, C. A., & Shafranske, E. P. (2004). *Clinical supervision: A competency-based approach.* Washington, D.C.: American Psychological Association.

Falender, C. A., & Shafranske, E. P. (2014). Clinical supervision: The state of the art. *Journal of Clinical Psychology, 70*(11), 1030–1041.

Forsberg, S., Fitzpatrick, K. K., Darcy, A., Aspen, V., Accurso, E. C., Bryson, S. W., . . . Lock, J. (2015). Development and evaluation of a treatment fidelity instrument for family-based treatment of adolescent anorexia nervosa. *International Journal of Eating Disorders, 48*(1), 91–99.

Hughes, E. K., Le Grange, D., Court, A., & Sawyer, S. M. (2017). A case series of family-based treatment for adolescents with atypical anorexia nervosa. *International Journal of Eating Disorders, 50*(4), 424–432.

Hughes, E. K., Le Grange, D., Court, A., Yeo, M., Campbell, S., Whitelaw, M., . . . Sawyer, S. M. (2014). Implementation of family-based treatment for adolescents with anorexia nervosa. *Journal of Pediatric Health Care, 28*(4), 322–330.

Kosmerly, S., Waller, G., & Robinson, A. L. (2015). Clinician adherence to guidelines in the delivery of family-based therapy for eating disorders. *International Journal of Eating Disorders, 48*(2), 223–229.

Le Grange, D., Lock, J., Agras, W. S., Bryson, S. W., & Jo, B. (2015). Randomized clinical trial of family-based treatment and cognitive-behavioral therapy for adolescent bulimia nervosa. *Journal of the American Academy of Child & Adolescent Psychiatry, 54*(11), 886–894.

Le Grange, D., Lock, J., Loeb, K., & Nicholls, D. (2010). Academy for eating disorders position paper: The role of the family in eating disorders. *International Journal of Eating Disorders, 43*(1), 1–5.

Lock, J., Agras, W. S., Bryson, S., & Kraemer, H. C. (2005). A comparison of short-and long-term family therapy for adolescent anorexia nervosa. *American Academy of Child and Adolescent Psychiatry, 44*(7), 632–639.

Lock, J., & Le Grange, D. (2015). *Treatment manual for anorexia nervosa: A family-based approach.* New York, NY: The Guilford Press.

Milne, D. (2009). *Evidence-based clinical supervision: Principles and practice.* West Sussex, UK: Blackwell.

Milne, D., & Dunkerley, C. (2010). Towards evidence-based clinical supervision: The development and evaluation of four CBT guidelines. *The Cognitive Behaviour Therapist, 3*(2), 43–57.

Milne, D., & Reiser, R. (2017). *A manual for evidence-based CBT supervision.* Hoboken, NJ: Wiley Blackwell.

Newman, C. F. (2013). Training cognitive behavioral therapy supervisors: Didactics, simulated practice, and "meta-supervision." *Journal of Cognitive Psychotherapy, 27*(1), 5–18.

Perepletchikova, F. (2011). On the topic of treatment integrity. *Clinical Psychology, 18*(2), 148–153.

Reiser, R. P., & Milne, D. (2012). Supervising cognitive-behavioral psychotherapy: Pressing needs, impressing possibilities. *Journal of Contemporary Psychotherapy, 42*(3), 161–171.

Walfish, S., McAlister, B., O'Donnell, P., & Lambert, M. J. (2012). An investigation of self-assessment bias in mental health providers. *Psychological Reports, 110*(2), 639–644.

2 Orientation to FBT Supervision
Notes From the Field

Sarah Forsberg, James Lock and Daniel Le Grange

The following guidelines were created with the assistance from advanced FBT supervisors and review of supervisory best practices. They are intended to provide a clear supervisory framework and many of the recommendations herein arise out of common challenges associated with acculturating FBT neophytes to the model. The process of orienting to FBT supervision mirrors the process of bringing families on board with the model as therapy is initiated. Just as one begins FBT with an orientation to the model, the rationale for the approach, expectations for the structure of treatment (within and across sessions) and focus of intervention, so too does the supervisor follow a similar orientation process in supervision.

Assessment Phase

The supervisor will first need to understand the background of the clinician to ascertain training needs and goals. Clinicians may come to the practice of FBT from wide-ranging avenues—some may be clinicians in graduate programs, and others may be seasoned and licensed clinicians who wish to grow in this area. Clinician background may have an impact on his or her motivations to do the work and potential challenges in learning and adhering to the treatment. For example, understanding clinicians' training may provide important information about the theoretical orientation of their previous training, which in some cases may not align well with FBT. The clinician needs to keep a developmental frame throughout the assessment of the training needs of each clinician being supervised (Stoltenberg & McNeill, 2010). During the process of acquiring a new skillset, early in supervision, clinicians are often trying to grasp main ideas underlying the treatment approach. Later supervision may focus on how individual clinicians can incorporate their personalities in delivering FBT interventions while still following the core tenets of FBT. Clinicians are likely ready for independent practice when they can find their own voice to comfortably deliver FBT interventions in a manner that is compatible with these tenets. In addition, they have the capacity to self-reflect, with awareness of where they may get stuck with families and how to use FBT strategies with more varied clinical presentations. Thus, prior to assigning cases to new clinicians, the supervisor spends time on assessment with the aim of conceptualizing the clinician in the context of his or her developmental stage more generally, and specifically in learning to treat eating disorders (ED) within the family-based model. Supervisors will seek to address early gaps in training that serve as prerequisites to doing FBT. Common gaps include having limited experience with eating disorders and never having worked with families, worked with a multidisciplinary team or managed medical issues. How a supervisor works with clinicians to fill these gaps in training will likely depend on the setting. For example, in some training programs didactics in these areas will have been conducted, but this will not always be the case. The supervisors' level of comfort with training on the ground will be dependent on a number of factors, including their capacity to provide this support and the background of the clinician.

Training Parameters

Prior to beginning FBT with a family, clinicians should have previously received some form of clinical training, given the specialized nature of eating disorders treatment and family work in general that requires a sophisticated skillset. Gathering this information helps the supervisor begin to formulate the developmental stage of the clinician. The supervisor will want to know whether the individual has had any prior exposure to FBT (perhaps being in a setting in which others around them are delivering the model) and to eating disorders. Basic prerequisites to beginning treatment with FBT include the 1.5-day Institute workshop, and reading the full treatment manual and seminal manuscripts detailing clinical outcomes. Other recommended readings include:

Help Your Teenager Beat an Eating Disorder by Lock and Le Grange
Eating Disorders in Children and Adolescents by Le Grange and Lock
Family Therapy for Adolescent Eating and Weight Disorders: New Applications by Loeb, Le Grange and Lock

For an entire list of resources, see Appendix I.

For many individuals who have limited background in these areas, spending time at the outset of supervision providing didactic training may be required to address any major misconceptions and gaps in the knowledge base. Clinicians are required to attend a 1.5-day training for FBT provided by certified trainers. Ideally, clinicians will have a strong foundational knowledge in eating disorders, including medical risks and standards for monitoring these, child and adolescent development, "nutrition 101" and the theoretical framework of FBT.

In addition to reviewing basic training requirements with the clinician, the following prompts (see also Appendix II) may serve as a guide to formalizing the assessment period of supervision:

1. Tell me about your prior training background. Have you worked with eating disorder populations? In what capacity? Do you have any prior training or exposure to FBT? In what setting?
2. What interests do you have in learning FBT? In working with families? In working with individuals with eating disorders?
3. What other treatment models/theoretical orientations have you received training in?
4. Have you done any previous treatment with families? Couples?
5. What do you hope to achieve in completing training in FBT? How do you see this experience fitting with your training and career goals?
6. What do you feel are your strengths as a clinician, and areas for growth?

From here, the supervisor will need to assess areas for additional training and work with the clinician to identify personalized training goals that map onto proficiency in FBT and in working with ED populations in general. For a list of resources clinicians might utilize in supporting filling gaps in training, see Appendix I.

The following vignette demonstrates what a supervisor might say to a new clinician to summarize the evidence base for FBT, highlighting important findings with an eye toward common misconceptions. For example, supervisors review empirical data with the clinician, highlighting key findings that may be relevant to planning for FBT.

At present, nine randomized clinical trials (RCTs) have been published comparing FBT to other treatment models (Agras et al., 2014; Eisler et al., 2000; Le Grange, Eisler, Dare, & Russell, 1992; Rhodes et al., 2008; Lock et al., 2010; Lock, Agras, Bryson, & Kraemer, 2005; Madden et al., 2015; Robin et al., 1999; Russell, Szmukler, Dare, & Eisler, 1987). FBT demonstrates better clinical outcomes than individual modalities, and these are maintained at one-year follow-up points (Le Grange et al., 2014; Lock et al., 2010). Rates of full remission defined as achieving 95% of median BMI and nonclinical levels of eating disorder symptomology (cognitions and behaviors) are around 33%–42% at end of treatment. Further, those in FBT are less likely to require hospitalization and to have relapsed at one-year posttreatment. When compared to a more traditional form of family therapy, individuals in FBT had more rapid weight gain and were less likely to be hospitalized (Agras et al., 2014). There are few indicators of who will respond best to FBT to guide decision making about when to use an alternative mode of treatment. Individuals who have a shorter duration of illness, or an age less than or onset prior to age

18, may fare better in FBT. Families who demonstrate high degrees of expressed emotion (high levels of criticism) have historically experienced greater benefit in a separated format of FBT (Rienecke, Accurso, Lock, & Le Grange, 2016).

Typically, FBT is delivered over a period of 6–12 months. Overall, there does not appear to be a significant benefit of a longer format, as individuals receiving a 10-session dose had equivalent outcomes to those meeting for 20 sessions (Lock, Couturier, & Agras, 2006). However, nonintact families and adolescents with greater obsessionality had better outcomes in the longer format. The strongest predictor of remission at end of treatment is early weight gain, specifically 4–5 lbs. within the first 4 weeks of treatment (Doyle, Le Grange, Loeb, Doyle, & Crosby, 2010; Le Grange, Accurso, Lock, Agras, & Bryson, 2014). Recent adaptations to address barriers when early weight restoration does not take place were examined, and these may help early non-responders get back on track (Lock et al., 2015).

Orientation to the Supervision Process

Following the assessment phase, supervisors then move to orienting to the process of supervision itself. Supervisors who subscribe to best practices of their profession and institution will utilize a supervision contract clearly outlining expectations (e.g., see American Psychological Association, 2015). Awareness of the content of such contracts at minimum will serve as a guide to supervisors in structuring their in-person orientation. These often include the following:

• Information on the content, method and context of supervision
• Responsibilities of the supervisor
• Expectations around clinician tasks and goals
• Methods of evaluation and expectations around competency
• Corrective processes
• Expectations around preparation for session and modes of observation
• Limits of confidentiality related to communications about clinician progress
• Expectations for clinician disclosures, legal and ethical parameters and their monitoring

Supervisors should be clear at the outset about their own supervisory style, which involves balancing personal preferences for the structuring of supervision, modes of teaching, and modes of providing and receiving feedback, for example, with best practices outlined in their profession and the requirements of their setting and recommended by this manual. Further, supervisors themselves should be self-reflective and consider their own cultural background, interpersonal style and learning experiences that shape their supervisory practice.

Supervisor Self-Assessment

In considering the ways in which we orient clinicians to the process of learning the FBT model, we recommend that supervisors take time to reflect on personal strengths and areas for growth in their role as supervisor. Perhaps this involves a review of feedback from clinicians, or taking time to complete a self-assessment. Use of this manual is meant to foster awareness of one's own supervisory style and enhance competency in this specialized domain. A central tenet in FBT is parental empowerment, whereby clinicians join parents in a collaborative process and transparency in thinking and problem solving is emphasized. Here again, we believe the process of FBT supervision should mirror these practices and, therefore, setting expectations at the outset of supervision is critical.

A Developmental Model of Supervision: Clinician Assessment and Learning

The developmental model of supervision is a common framework integrated into many training contexts—for example, the APA uses developmental benchmarks to assess a clinician's progression toward independent practice (McNeill & Stoltenberg, 2016; Stoltenberg & McNeill, 2010). In this way, clinicians progress from requiring significant guidance and teaching, with a focus on the mechanics of an intervention, toward increasingly subtle, complex and integrative ways of thinking about cases and their own unique delivery of prescribed interventions. As the supervisory relationship is forming, it is important to integrate the information gathered about the clinicians' training trajectory into a "formulation" of the training goals and developmental stage of the clinician. Making this explicit is recommended. For those who have not previously conducted FBT, their awareness of strengths and areas for growth within the context of this treatment model will not be well conceptualized at the outset. Thus, in the early stages of supervision, the supervisor may look for and highlight where the clinician grasps concepts and where there are opportunities for self-reflection and growth. These observations are best made explicit using directly observable, behavioral data. It is not useful when these data appear to "come out of the blue," for example, and instead should be framed in the context of learning objectives. To solidify a framework for providing feedback, best practice involves providing the clinician with a copy of the assessment benchmarks up front. This not only increases transparency in the supervision relationship but also provides an opportunity for clinicians to engage in a self-reflective process that directs their focus toward learning goals specific to FBT.

Another marker of clinician development is the ability to formulate questions that are diagnostic of the challenges arising in the session. For example, early-stage clinicians are more likely to give a summary of the session and highlight areas of confusion, and at times may be subject to providing a dis-organized and diffuse report of the session. This may reflect early efforts to grasp the complexity of the model, or for more advanced clinicians can also reflect a response that is atypical and perhaps diagnostic of family complexi-ties or differences.

When assessing developmental stage, The supervisor is looking for:

- How does the clinician understand current dilemmas in the broader con-ceptualization of the family and eating disorder, and place in treatment?
- Are they still learning the model/adherence or are they asking higher-level questions?
- Is the language they use reflective of FBT philosophy?
- Does their language reflect understanding of relevant interventions?

The supervisor is looking for these points of growth and observing them openly with the clinician—for example, "*Your question about addressing barriers to parental meal monitoring is in line with where things would be in Phase I.*" In addition, they are looking at Broad clinician competency:

- Strengths and weaknesses that can come with doing FBT and working with families and an ED population more broadly
- The ability to self-reflect and acknowledge stuck points and indica-tors of growth

Orientation to the Structure of Supervision

After obtaining additional background on the clinician to identify devel-opmental stage and related goals, the supervisor begins by discussing the structure (logistics and processes) of supervision. For example, the supervi-sor must determine whether supervision will be conducted in a group or individual format, whether supervision will occur at a set time each week, the duration of supervision (which will depend on the format, and number of cases), modes of observation, and preferences around contact outside of supervision. Supervisors may require some level of live supervision, whether it is through a one-way mirror, sitting in on early sessions or review of audio or videotape. We highly recommend some form of in vivo observation early on in training as it enriches the learning process and solves the problems of poor memory recall and tendency for clinicians to be overly attentive to mistakes and challenges or alternatively influenced by self-protective distor-tion and biases (Haggerty & Hilsenroth, 2011). In fact, live review of ses-sions has been linked to improved clinician and patient outcomes in some treatments (Haggerty & Hilsenroth, 2011). Ahead we provide guidelines on how to engage in review of live (video or audiotaped sessions). When there is no format for direct observation, the supervisor orients to the structure of case presentation to provide greater focus for supervision questions and dilemmas. Supervisors and clinicians alike will benefit from communication around the structure of case presentation; thus the following anchors may serve as a helpful guide as they track progress in supervision.

Guideline for Case Presentation in Supervision

In service of most efficiently utilizing time in supervision and identifying key opportunities for intervention, we encourage clinicians to come prepared with a case formulation and framing questions. This is an important part of the learning process for clinicians who are asked to organize their thinking about cases in a way that is consistent with the model. Rehearsal of step-by-step interventions is a mechanism for enhancing learning at early stages. When setting the supervisory agenda, clinicians may be encouraged to present their specific questions and the supervisor listens for opportunities to refine their questions or perhaps identifies other, important questions that could highlight gaps in knowledge of the model and potential areas for additional teaching. A framing question/dilemma is a succinct description of the stated problem/dilemma. Some examples of such questions include:

> *"I need help figuring out what is preventing Mom from showing up consistently for sessions."*
> *"I haven't felt successful in joining the family and am uncertain about the barriers."*
> *"I am noticing that members of the medical team have been communicating recommendations to family that I believe are inconsistent with FBT and our current focus—can you help me figure out how to approach this issue with them?"*

At times, especially when newer to the treatment model, clinicians may need assistance in determining a specific question. Further, there may be cases that feel "stuck," and the clinician really needs help formulating the problem before identifying solutions. In this case, the framing dilemma/question might be something like:

> *"I feel stuck and need help figuring out why,"* or *"I know I'm struggling with this case but I'm not sure what specific questions I need help with."* In these cases, the supervisor leaves additional space for the clinician to outwardly process his or her dilemma while listening for any themes that might guide a conceptualization of the current challenge. We find that reliance on framing questions prevents situations in which supervisors might end up trying to solve an unrelated problem, clinicians feel they aren't being heard or the true issue remains unresolved.

Case Presentation Guide for FBT (Appendix III)

The following family assessment tool is a guide to help the clinician gather and reflect on relevant family information, and assist in conceptualizing the case. This provides a foundation for identifying family challenges (e.g., illness maintaining behaviors), strengths and other potential barriers to progress to be aware of as treatment progresses.

Family and adolescent presenting information

Name
Age
Family constitution: who is in the family, who attends
sessions, relevant family background—mental health
history, family transitions, separations, losses, family
cultural background
Summary of eating disorder history
Duration of illness: brief description of evolution of
ED behavior
Current height/weight/BMI percentile:
Weight history:
Highest BMI for age percentile
Weight at highest BMI for age percentile
Lowest BMI for age percentile
Weight at lowest BMI for age percentile
**Previous treatment history, including comorbid
conditions**
Hypotheses on family maintaining behaviors:
imbalance in family structure, parental conflict
around approach, beliefs about the illness that inform
intervention
Family strengths

Recommendations for Review of Audio or Videotapes

- Early in supervision, supervisors watch a few sessions in their entirety (Session 1, 2, another Phase I, II and III session at minimum). From this point onward, as the clinician has specific questions about moments in the session, he or she may be required by the supervisor to cue the session in advance.

- When there is a specific question, or the supervisor identifies an opportunity for teaching, watching the portion of video together in session is an important intervention. This provides opportunity for the feedback to be specific, and for role-plays that are directly relevant to the family.

- Often supervisors may have difficulty sifting through the many opportunities for feedback, especially with developmentally early clinicians. In this case, the supervisor should focus on teaching to the primary tenets of FBT. They may identify 2–3 themes that decrease fidelity, introduce the FBT tenet, why it is important, and follow up with a specific example in session that requires adjustment to increase adherence.

- As noted, the supervisor will rely on the clinician to engage in increasingly sophisticated self-reflection, preparing portions of videotapes in advance for review. The supervisor encourages the clinician to identify a specific question that highlights his or her consideration of FBT and potential barriers to effective implementation.

- The supervisor encourages the clinician to identify strategies for incorporating feedback. The supervisor and clinician may keep a detailed log of supervision, and the clinician may be asked to provide a summary at the end of the supervision session demonstrating tasks to focus on in upcoming sessions.

Evaluating Progress

The evaluative process of supervision should be transparent and discussed in the context of the supervisory contract. Some settings (e.g., accredited academic training institutions) will require a specific evaluation instrument to be utilized at specified time points in the training, and supervisors should review these documents when supervision begins. This process also provides an opportunity for clinicians to self-reflect on strengths and areas for growth as they relate to these specific benchmarks, and may facilitate more detailed goal setting and plans for monitoring throughout. For example, the recent development of a fidelity tool to monitor clinician adherence and competence in FBT interventions has been included to provide clinicians and supervisors a reference point to ensure understanding and acquisition of the model.

Supervision Tracking Form (Appendix IV)

The following is a form that supervisors may use to guide their monitoring of clinician cases. Most governing bodies require that supervisors document their recommendations in supervision in the event there is need to review the case. Supervisors should review guidelines associated with their specific licensing body.

In addition, you will find a form clinicians can utilize during therapy to guide their own patient tracking in Appendix IV. This form is meant to aid in providing an overview of patient progress, prepare clinicians for supervision and consultation and ensure patients are on track. The form has a place for clinicians to fill out dates for a 4-week review, in keeping with the aim of identifying those who have not had a good response (>4 lbs. of weight gain in the first 4 weeks of therapy), and 4-month review (to ensure patients are nearing weight restoration (~90%–95% of expected body weight) and are moving toward Phase III of treatment.

Supervision Tracking Form (Appendix IV)

Supervision Date:

Current Session # and Phase:

Weight Progress:

Any significant safety/legal/ethical issues needing immediate attention?

How was the session structured—what FBT-specific interventions occurred?

Did any not occur that should have? Why?

Family barriers and strengths—is the clinician tracking these?

What are common supervision questions and related training/competency issues?

A Brief Primer on Modes of Teaching

The following modes of teaching in supervision are taken from an evidence-based model of supervision (Milne, 2009; Milne & Reiser, 2017). These strategies are grouped as follows: *symbolic* (i.e., words, as in case presentation), *iconic* (i.e., images, such as watching a tape) or *enactive* (i.e., actions, like role play).

Symbolic

• Case presentation

  • Clinician practices presentation of relevant case data and an FBT-congruent formulation.

• Questioning and challenging: Asking, "What would you do next?"

  • Clinicians can be reminded that this is an opportunity to draw out their thinking about cases and they are not expected to know the answer early on. It is important to reinforce clinicians for taking risks, especially early on.

• Instruction/teaching/informing/suggestion

  • The supervisor provides direct feedback/suggestions, drawing on research literature or referencing the treatment manual or cases that have encountered similar challenges.

- Planning

  - The supervisor will guide the clinician to identify an action plan for the subsequent family therapy session and encourage the clinician to summarize next steps at the end of the session.

- Facilitating self-reflection ("What might have you done differently?")

  - Developing the self-reflective muscle in supervision is important. The clinician may be asked to explore his or her responses to a family that led to a specific response.

- Tips and examples from supervisor's clinical experiences

  - This is an opportunity to normalize the clinicians' challenges as many of the themes addressed in this manual are included due to their commonality.

- Feedback/evaluation (what worked, what didn't)

  - Feedback should reflect directly observable behaviors and may be delivered most effectively through including reinforcing underlying positive intentions, normalizing typical pitfalls and balancing with reflection of points of progress.

Iconic

- Modeling by supervisor, demonstrating using video

  - The supervisor may rehearse what he or she would say in response to a specific family communication. The supervisor may also provide examples of video of interventions delivered with high levels of competency.

- Observation of clinician (sitting in, co-therapy)

  - In some settings, the clinician may observe a more senior clinician/ supervisor in action.

- Joint observation and commenting on clinician's performance recorded on audio or videotape

Enactive

- Role play (Socratic questioning)

  - Typically, a clinician will be asked to provide some background to the supervisor about the challenge that is leading him or her to feel stuck.
  - First, the supervisor will play the clinician, with the clinician taking the role of the family member.

- Following the role play, the supervisor will ask the clinician if he or she felt he or she was able to capture the challenge, and how the clinician thinks the family would respond to the supervisor's intervention.
- The clinician should be encouraged to request a continuation of the role play if he or she continues to feel stuck.
- Finally, the clinician should summarize what he or she felt worked, how it diverged from his or her interventions, and why, and his or her confidence in being able to try this intervention on his or her own.

- Behavioral experiments

  - The supervisor may assist the clinician in identifying a hypothesis about the maintaining variables of a family behavior. Subsequently, they would together identify ways of shifting the session, specific questions to ask that would assist the clinician in obtaining additional data to confirm/disconfirm the hypothesis.

- Live supervision (observes and actively advises during session)

  - Historically in family therapy sessions supervision involved the use of one-way mirrors to assist new clinicians and also to provide a more objective perspective existing outside of the family system.

- Learning exercises

  - The clinician might be asked to read scientific articles that address specific questions.
  - The clinician may be asked to generate a list of circular questions to address his or her hypotheses.

Supervision Roadmap

Moving forward, we will highlight various common dilemmas that arise in FBT for discussion in supervision. The following framework is designed to serve as a guide as you approach your supervision sessions.

- Diagnose the dilemma.

  a. What key tenets of FBT apply in the identified scenario?
  b. What interventions are being left out?
  c. Were there any interventions that were delivered incompletely? Or possibly misinterpreted and delivered in a fashion incongruent with the model?
  d. What is the clinician's question (is there a question), and does this represent the dilemma or is there another underlying issue that needs to be formulated?

- Frame the dilemma and the question back to the clinician to ensure accurate interpretation of the data presented.

- Identify learning needs, which may be related to:

    a. Adherence to specific interventions and competency in their delivery
    b. Gaps in general knowledge (e.g., about eating disorders, weight targets)
    c. Stylistic or process-oriented challenges

- Identify possible teaching modalities that match the problem-solving needs of the situation and clinician developmental needs (see modes of teaching ahead).
- May utilize 2–3 different modes of teaching to match clinician needs.

It is recommended that supervisors first tailor their interventions to the clinician's developmental level. A supervisor who provides only didactic feedback and suggestions may be ineffective in helping more advanced clinicians grow, as they may already have the capacity to do these things on their own, for example. Combining 2–3 methods may actually be more effective than using just one, as it will allow for approaching challenges from multiple angles and provide both parties with an opportunity to identify what was helpful in moving the clinician forward and why.

Case Example

In this case, the clinician beginning FBT had a strong history of individual therapy experience, which was explored during the initial assessment phase of supervision. At the outset of supervision, the new learning opportunities and challenges associated with shifting to a family focus were reviewed. As anticipated, both the supervisor and clinician jointly reflected the ongoing challenge the clinician faced in overfocusing on the needs of the adolescent, at times leading the clinician to question parental authority. Here the supervisor shared this observation with the clinician by:

- Providing concrete examples when this was observed to take place (here the clinician shared in session that "*The family seems to have no sympathy for their daughter when she cries, they are quite rejecting of her and ignore her concerns—no wonder she shuts down.*"
- Revisiting the objective to move their concerns for the adolescent into the family context and become comfortable with managing these familial processes in the session (a goal identified at the outset).
- Identifying means of strengthening adherence to FBT principles (e.g., how externalization and redirection of criticism might be used effectively).
- Helping the clinician identify the potential learning opportunities inherent in this experience in the context of his or her goals.

Using this framework, the supervisor is likely to maintain receptivity to feedback, and thus provide concrete data to support the need to strengthen a skillset. In this case the supervisor said, "*We have talked previously about the differences between individual and family therapy, specifically the challenges that arise in addressing conflict that come about in the session between family members and balancing validation of adolescents and their parents. I have been noticing in the last few meetings you have expressed your own frustration at your patient's parents, and in your retelling of the session I hear a desire to validate the adolescent to counter the family's criticism.*" The supervisor then provided a specific example forming the basis of this observation.

At this point, the supervisor asked the clinician to engage in self-reflection by asking if this feedback fit with his or her experience. When the clinician agreed and elaborated on his or her reaction, the supervisor proceeded by saying, "*At times, this may lead to a reinforcement of eating disorder behaviors and/or parental guilt. What we are going to focus on here is how to both express interest and empathy for your patient while not aligning with their illness. I would like for us to explore how we can model for the parents a new and more effective way of responding to their daughter's distress at the hands of AN. When we think about the core principles of FBT, where do you feel you, and the parents, are getting stuck?*"

The clinician's ability to respond to such feedback is also likely to reflect his or her developmental level, representing his or her awareness of personal reactions based on values, viewpoints and prior training, and his or her intersection with knowledge of the treatment. From there, the supervisor and clinician engaged in a role play to identify potential responses to particularly difficult family criticism with a focus on practicing the language of externalization.

References

Agras, W. S., Lock, J., Brandt, H., Bryson, S. W., Dodge, E., Halmi, K. A., . . . Woodside, B. (2014). Comparison of 2 family therapies for adolescent anorexia nervosa: A randomized parallel trial, *JAMA Psychiatry, 71*(11), 1279–1286.

American Psychological Association. (2015). Guidelines for clinical supervision in health service psychology. *American Psychologist, 70*(1), 33–46.

Doyle, P. M., Le Grange, D., Loeb, K., Doyle, A. C., & Crosby, R. D. (2010). Early response to family-based treatment for adolescent anorexia nervosa. *International Journal of Eating Disorders, 43*(7), 659–662.

Eisler, I., Dare, C., Hodes, M., Russell, G., Dodge, E., & Le Grange, D. (2000). Family therapy for adolescent anorexia nervosa: The results of a controlled comparison of two family interventions. *Journal of Child Psychology and Psychiatry, and Allied Disciplines, 41*(6), 727–736.

Haggerty, G., & Hilsenroth, M., J. (2011). The use of video in psychotherapy supervision. *British Journal of Psychotherapy, 27*(2), 193–210.

Le Grange, D., Accurso, E. C., Lock, J., Agras, S., & Bryson, S. W. (2014). Early weight gain predicts outcome in two treatments for adolescent anorexia Nervosa. *International Journal of Eating Disorders*, 47(2), 124–129.

Le Grange, D., Eisler, I., Dare, C., & Russell, G. F. M. (1992). Evaluation of family treatments in adolescent anorexia nervosa: A pilot study. *International Journal of Eating Disorders*, 12(4), 347–357.

Le Grange, D., Lock, J., Accurso, E. C., Agras, W. S., Darcy, A., Forsberg, S., & Bryson, S. W. (2014). Relapse from remission at two- to four-year follow-up in two treatments for adolescent anorexia nervosa. *Journal of the American Academy of Child and Adolescent Psychiatry*, 53(11), 1162–1167.

Lock, J., Agras, W. S., Bryson, S., & Kraemer, H. C. (2005). A comparison of short-and long-term family therapy for adolescent anorexia nervosa. *American Academy of Child and Adolescent Psychiatry*, 44(7), 632–639.

Lock, J., Couturier, J., & Agras, W. S. (2006). Comparison of long-term outcomes in adolescents with anorexia nervosa treated with family therapy. *Journal of the American Academy of Child & Adolescent Psychiatry*, 45(6), 666–672.

Lock, J., Le Grange, D., Agras, W. S., Kara, K., Jo, B., Accurso, E., . . . Arnow, K. (2015). Can adaptive treatment improve outcomes in family-based therapy for adolescents with anorexia nervosa? Feasibility and treatment effects of a multi-site treatment study. *Behaviour Research and Therapy*, 73, 90–95.

Lock, J., Le Grange, D., Agras, W. S., Moye, A., Bryson, S. W., & Jo, B. (2010). Randomized clinical trial comparing family-based treatment with adolescent-focused individual therapy for adolescents with anorexia nervosa. *Archives of General Psychiatry*, 67(10), 1025–1032.

Madden, S., Miskovic-Wheatley, J., Wallis, A., Kohn, M., Lock, J., Le Grange, D., . . . Touyz, S. (2015). A randomized controlled trial of in-patient treatment for anorexia nervosa in medically unstable adolescents. *Psychological Medicine*, 45(2), 415–427.

McNeill, B. W., & Stoltenberg, C. D. (2016). *Supervision essentials for the integrative developmental model* (1st ed.). Washington, DC: American Psychological Association.

Milne, D. (2009). *Evidence-based clinical supervision: Principles and practice.* West Sussex, UK: Blackwell.

Milne, D., & Reiser, R. P. (2017). *A manual for evidence-based CBT supervision.* Hoboken, NJ: Wiley Blackwell.

Rhodes, P., Baillee, A., Brown, J., & Madden, S. (2008). Can parent-to-parent consultation improve the effectiveness of the Maudsley model of family-based treatment for anorexia nervosa? A randomized control trial. *Journal of Family Therapy*, 30(1), 96–108.

Rienecke, R. D., Accurso, E. C., Lock, J., & Le Grange, D. (2016). Expressed emotion, family functioning, and treatment outcome for adolescents with anorexia nervosa. *European Eating Disorders Review*, 24(1), 43–51.

Robin, A. L., Siegel, P. T., Moye, A. W., Gilroy, M., Dennis, A. B., & Sikand, A. (1999). A controlled comparison of family versus individual therapy for adolescents with anorexia nervosa. *Journal of the American Academy of Child & Adolescent Psychiatry*, 38(12), 1482–1489.

Russell, G., Szmukler, G., Dare, C., & Eisler, I. (1987). An evaluation of family therapy in anorexia nervosa and bulimia nervosa. *Archives of General Psychiatry*, 44(12), 1047–1056.

Stoltenberg, C. D., & McNeill, B. W. (2010). *IDM supervision: The integrative developmental model of supervision* (3rd ed.). New York: Routledge.

3 Beginning Well

Sarah Forsberg, James Lock and Daniel Le Grange

FBT begins with the first contact with the family. In these early stages, the supervisor is focused on assisting the clinician in setting a clear framework for treatment, building rapport and engaging the family, and providing a rationale for the approach. How one frames treatment at the outset will impact the tone of work with the family throughout treatment. To prepare the clinician evaluates:

*   Is the family ready to put AN first?
*   Can the adults in the picture agree that this is an approach they need to use and can they put their differences aside to use this approach?
*   Does the family know that in pursuing treatment, they may need to put other aspects of their life on hold? That they may need to take time away from work and reduce commitments with other children in order to give their child the care he or she needs?

Initial Assessment

The following learning tasks associated with engaging the family are embedded and discussed throughout the remainder of this chapter. For additional guidance on these topics, specific references are provided.

*   Engaging the family in a phone call
*   Creating a focus on family treatment
*   How to include the entire family
*   Assessing medical urgency and current level of medical monitoring
*   Getting comfortable in the role of team leader and orienting family members to team member roles

    *   Associated reading: *The Role of the Pediatrician in Family-Based Treatment for Adolescent Eating Disorders: Opportunities and Challenges* (Katzman, Peebles, Sawyer, Lock, & Le Grange, 2013)

*   Helping clinicians understand the core principle of parental empowerment

Common Dilemmas

Our intention in outlining common dilemmas supervisors may face in teaching the model to clinicians is that you will hold these in mind in your beginning discussions with clinicians. These early phases may often require additional didactic learning. The manual also outlines these common early difficulties and provides advice on how to proceed. Here, the focus is on:

- Identifying gaps in learning
- The process of teaching
- Identifying potential clinician barriers to successful implementation
- Utilizing various supervision strategies to match the clinician's needs

Understanding Parental Empowerment

Description of the Challenge

Parental empowerment as a concept refers to positioning parents to make autonomous decisions regarding their child's care. They are not reliant upon prescriptions from the treatment team to make decisions on issues of renourishment. The focus of this empowerment, then, should be tied with parental responsibility to act, as well as engaging parents in solving the problem of renourishment.

Many individuals struggle with stylistic strategies to promote parental empowerment, which often stems from a misinterpretation of the concept. It is not uncommon for clinicians early in training to take an *overly passive* or *overly directive* stance with families. In addition, families often do not understand this concept and should be assisted in understanding their role, as this is quite a shift from traditional models of psychotherapy. Supervisors should be listening for indications that clinicians do not fully grasp this concept and therefore have trouble assisting families in understanding them as well. For example, it is not uncommon for clinicians to respond to family concerns about renourishment with statements such as, "*I'm confident you'll find a way to work it out*," in the absence of supporting family solution generating and problem solving. Instead, it is best to guide the family to identifying the specific challenges they are facing, while contributing information where there are gaps in knowledge. We often state that families have their own experience of their family and of the eating disorder (or the ED), but they have only their one child and could not be expected to have a broader understanding. It is the clinician's job to put this broader and specific information in context and provide the information that is relevant but missing so families can generalize to meet their own needs.

It is important to emphasize that parental empowerment does not mean that parents have all of the answers (and if they did, they would be successfully refeeding their child without a treatment team!). Further, as we often remind parents, conceptualizing eating disorders (ED) falls well outside the bounds of a "parenting 101" handbook. Thus, while parents may present with many ideas based on their own knowledge of mental illness, conceptualization of what treatment should include, and cultural attitudes toward mental illness, families are unlikely to be familiar with EDs or FBT. In this respect, clinicians *are* the experts, and regardless of whether they are advanced in their training or novice, they must develop comfort in embodying this role. Many feel that they lack skills to help the family understand the medical and psychological sequelae of this disease, or to assist parents with renourishment. This is often a place where clinicians become stuck. Lack of confidence is often part of the problem and for some, ironically, may lead to the clinician taking an overly directive stance with families, and miss opportunities to reinforce the skills and knowledge families have at the outset of treatment. For others, clinicians may become passive, asking families to carry responsibility for decision making that is outside of their current skillset. Other challenges include reverting to methods with which the clinician is more comfortable, such as providing feedback from a cognitive-behavioral approach or too much emphasis on trying to engage the adolescent patient and/or attempting to gain patient compliance. Assisting clinicians in learning the nuances of the dance between actively attuning to family perspectives and strengths, reinforcing healthy decision making, and setting clear expectations around treatment tasks and goals is key.

Supervisory Intervention

The following strategies may assist supervisors in guiding clinicians' understanding of this concept. First, the supervisor seeks to help the clinician understand his or her role in the family context. The supervisor may draw parallels between the clinician role and the role of a consultant, saying,

> *You are an expert on eating disorders and how to best treat these illnesses— families likely have little to no prior experience with eating disorders. Thus, your role is one of confidante and expert consultant to the parents in their efforts to reverse starvation. At the same time, you will balance this role with an awareness of parental expertise in knowing their child—they have watched their child grow and evolve into who they are today and have a rich narrative to share. At times, it may seem as though yours and the family's perspectives may be in conflict and it is your job to bring them together to help the family form a new narrative around the ways in which the eating disorder has coopted their ability to fully know their child as they are currently covered by their illness.*

Helping the clinician conceptualize his or her role by using an illustrative example may be helpful in supporting the intricate dance between directing and facilitating parental empowerment.

Encouraging Articulation of Family Strengths

The supervisor may directly elicit the clinician's assessment of family strengths at the outset of treatment. This may prompt discussion of how family skills are being thwarted by the illness, which presents an opportunity for additional instruction by the clinician. This can also be understood by following the steps it took for the family to initiate treatment, arrange their schedules and arrive for treatment. These actions took focus, problem solving, coordination and follow-through on the part of the family, and the clinician can be directed to highlight these strengths throughout treatment to identify ways the family may use these strengths toward new challenges.

Areas that are important for supervisors and clinicians to review to increase their understanding of family strengths include: the facility of scheduling the appointment/length of time between referral and scheduling (if known), family presence and timeliness at initial sessions, and family follow-up with the medical team or other recommended providers. Aspects that can be assessed for strengths include family and partner communication, flexibility, planning, problem solving, persistence, focus, resiliency, use of humor, resources (education, job, availability), supportiveness of siblings, historical ability to overcome problems and parental communication. For example, a family who has an intact parental unit who has historically communicated well about other challenges, is already skilled in authoritative parenting and has social supports in the area is going to feel quite different than a single-parent family with multiple siblings and limited social support.

Evaluating the Extent of Parental Empowerment and Potential Impediments

Some families present to treatment in an extremely disempowered state, which may be due to misinformation, previous experiences of feeling blamed for their child's illness, and feelings of hopelessness around their ability to intervene. Completing this review sets the frame for active problem solving with the clinician around their ability to draw on other interventions designed to enhance parental empowerment (e.g., reducing parental blame, an agnostic stance, externalization of illness).

The Family Assessment

Key aspects of the family assessment include:

- Information obtained in initial contacts with the family

  - How did the family mobilize—were there barriers they had to overcome? How effective/efficient were they in overcoming these?

- Information Obtained in Session 1

  - What language do the parents use at the outset? How confident do the parents appear and does their confidence match steps they have taken to address their child's dilemma?

- How quickly did the family respond once the problem had been identified?
- What sorts of barriers were there to acting on the problem of AN (lack of communication, closeness—e.g., "We don't really eat meals together")?
- How do parents respond to the directive to take responsibility for refeeding? Do they appear reluctant, resigned, actively against or eager to enact this role?
- What type of planning behavior do the parents demonstrate at the end of the session? Do they express an understanding of their role in refeeding as it relates to the period of time between sessions?

- Information Obtained Between Sessions

  - How often are the parents reaching out to the clinician/other members of the treatment team in between sessions?
  - What kinds of questions are they identifying?
  - Do their questions/concerns reflect underlying anxiety about their capabilities, confusion about the illness, how to respond or lack of confidence in the treatment team/model?

Modeling the Nuances of Discussions With Families to Promote Empowerment

The supervisor may provide direct examples of the kind of language they may use to facilitate empowerment—for example, "While you know how important it is for your daughter to be engaged with peers at school, back to playing soccer, you also recognize that until she is rid of this eating disorder it (the eating disorder) will continue to take these (activities/interests) away from her."

Engaging the Self-Reflective Process

At times clinicians' own emotional reactions to a family may be an impediment. For example, they may experience anxiety around their ability to engage families, may fall into the pit of despair with families joining them in their hopelessness, or may harbor their own feelings of criticism and blame toward parental behaviors. Early in supervision, as comfort and safety are in development, the supervisor may take this opportunity to engage in *modeling* self-reflection, modeling an awareness of his or her own historical reactions to families. For example, a supervisor might reflect on his or her own reactions to hearing the case presentation, with a focus on how these experiences have manifested and impacted early treatment decisions with other families. Early modeling sets the expectation that clinicians are fallible and human, and can glean important information about families through observation of nuances in their reaction. As clinicians advance in their training, these sorts of discussions often no longer need to be elicited if the modeling has the desired effect of shaping the clinician's thinking about their own process, with a specific focus on why certain familial patterns or behaviors may provoke modifications to the treatment framework. Common concerns that arise and impact fidelity tend to be related to working with divorced families, parent eating disorders, issues of difference or diversity—cultural, economic, sexuality, religious preference—and parental beliefs about food/eating.

The following review of evidence may provide a framework for discussing these potential preexisting beliefs about the types of families likely to benefit from FBT. To date, the research does not provide evidence suggesting that certain family variables are exclusionary to working in FBT. Some data suggests that nonintact families take longer to respond (Lock, Agras, Bryson, & Kraemer, 2005). If clinicians have bias, this may impact their confidence and diminish efforts at parental empowerment. Preliminary data suggest that higher parental self-efficacy and early increases in self-efficacy are predictive of a better outcome (Byrne, Accurso, Arnow, Lock, & Grange, 2015).

Taking on the task of refeeding requires a significant commitment on the part of parents. In our experience, most parents, regardless of resources (e.g., economic, social), are highly motivated to do what it takes to help their child. Instead of deciding when a family faces insurmountable barriers, the clinician facilitates a discussion to elicit the challenges inherent in the parents' current situation. For example, in the case of working with divorced or single parents, the clinician will work with parents to identify possible additional supports (other family members, community supports, including friends, church members, school personnel). When working with divorced families, clinicians will help parents assess their willingness and ability to work together, or alternatively, may recommend one parent take primary responsibility for meal supervision/monitoring while the other parent assists in navigating other supports and logistical challenges.

Beliefs about family cultural background may also come into play, and reflect common stereotypes/prejudice or lack of exposure to working with specific cultural groups. These concerns most often arise in the context of how families have been impacted by mental health stigma and may reflect cultural beliefs about mental health conditions and treatment, or systemic oppression of certain groups by the medical and therapeutic community, for example. Further, cultural beliefs may be informed by parental history of mental health challenges, including parental history of an ED. Clinicians should be encouraged to reflect on their own beliefs and experiences so they may differentiate these from the realized barriers families are facing. In FBT, we begin with the following family assumptions: families are resilient, have unique strengths and challenges (and are doing the best they can given current circumstances) and are at baseline motivated to help their child. Taking this stance allows for greater flexibility and freedom in exploring potential barriers to engagement *as they arise* in assessment and early treatment. If there are concerns about a family's ability to undertake the task of FBT, families should be prompted to reflect on these and make an informed decision through review of benefits/risks and alternatives.

Unfortunately, to date there is limited research on the impact of cultural variables, specifically with regards to ethnicity, race, immigration status or fluency in the dominant cultural language, for example. In our clinical experience, families from a wide variety of backgrounds can benefit from FBT when clinicians strive to become culturally competent, approach families with open-mindedness and are able to truly join families in making the treatment work for them. Research on treatment engagement and outcome is sorely lacking in this area and future studies may help shed light on whether specific cultural considerations or modifications can improve outcomes in FBT. In current clinical practice, supervisors strive to support clinicians in examining their own cultural background as it relates to issues of implicit bias and stereotypes that are at interplay with any given family. Further discussion on this topic can be found in Chapter 10.

Another area in which little is yet known is the influence of parental psychopathology in FBT. What we do know is that caring for a child with an ED is associated with significant stress and caregiver burden (Kyriacou, Treasure, & Schmidt, 2008; Zabala, Macdonald, & Treasure, 2009). Further, a recent study examining parent symptomology in FBT suggests a low rate of parent psychopathology at baseline, and that these symptoms decrease over treatment and do not appear to be predictive of treatment outcome (Forsberg et al., 2015).

Keeping the Therapeutic Focus in the Face of Family Concerns

Description of the Challenge

As noted, challenges to parental empowerment often arise in the context of family assertion that they know best, and strong opinions about the way in which they would like treatment to proceed (e.g., asking to exclude a family member, desire for additional forms of treatment, wanting to attend less frequently). In these instances it is most helpful for clinicians to have a strong understanding of the theoretical rationale for FBT and potential for these disruptions to the treatment frame to undermine engagement and progress.

Supervisory Intervention

EARLY DIDACTICS ON COMMON CHALLENGES IN MAINTAINING
THE TREATMENT FRAME

The supervisor helps to preview challenges associated with managing the treatment frame and problem-solve in advance around how to manage these in supervision.

With a novice clinician, the supervisor will model, using his or her own language, a typical response to some of these family dilemmas—for example:

- Parents want to leave a sibling out (they are concerned about the impact it will have on the sibling)

    - *Each member of the family is a vital part of your child's support, and just as each of you has been impacted differently by this illness, each has a slightly different role to fill in supporting your son's recovery. In FBT, siblings are there to help your child in his struggle by providing support, nurturance and a sense of normalcy. Further, I imagine your daughter is experiencing a range of confusing emotions in response to the changes in her brother. By better understanding what her brother is going through, we find that siblings are likely to feel better and more empowered to be a support.*

- Parents request individual therapy to address eating disorder symptoms or perceived/actual comorbidities:

    - *I'm noticing you have many reservations about proceeding in FBT. The foremost concerns you shared include wanting your child to have additional individual support and that we are not currently focused on treating her anxiety. As we have discussed, we do not recommend that patients participate in individual therapy and FBT simultaneously. Patients often struggle to use psychotherapy effectively when malnourished and it is generally not successful to do two treatments at the same time. If your daughter was receiving treatment for cancer, for example, her treatment team might recommend surgery first prior to determining a need for chemotherapy. Similarly, in FBT, we need to help restore healthy brain functioning to determine the need to address underlying anxiety, which requires significant mental effort and motivation. I am wondering what it would take to be able to put these concerns aside temporarily, knowing that we will be carefully monitoring her anxiety coming back as needed as she is healthier.*

- If parents have difficulty accepting this rationale and request to put these concerns on hold, the clinician might say,

    It seems as though I have not been effective in alleviating your concerns and we are stuck and unable to move forward. If there are any other questions I can answer for you, I am happy to; however, perhaps we should revisit alternative treatments and their likely outcome. The foremost requirement of participating in FBT is agreeing to the treatment and its effectiveness is based on our ability to stay focused. Your commitment is what will make this treatment successful, and if you aren't sure this is the approach for you we should not proceed until we've explored your concerns further. At the same time, the longer we take to make a commitment, the more time and space we allow for the eating disorder to continue to set its teeth into your daughter.

In some cases, clinicians may have worked to address parental concerns, and despite best efforts families may continue to struggle with the structure and requirements of the treatment. Supervisors may ask clinicians to practice role-playing these conversations, to first recreate the conversation, second identify points of challenge and third generate a new approach that adequately addresses challenges. For further guidance, supervisors may utilize the role-play guideline found (Modes of Teaching) in Chapter 2.

Taking a Leadership Role in Team Communications

Description of the Challenge

When treating eating disorders, clinicians will need to learn how to collaborate with the broader treatment team. In some instances, members of the team have different backgrounds, training and philosophies about the etiology and treatment of eating disorders. Especially given the level of medical acuity associated with these illnesses, clinicians must be comfortable managing these risks and develop a relationship with other team members to provide the best care. In many cases, early clinicians may defer to other medical providers, who if they are not educated in FBT can potentially interfere with efforts at parental empowerment and may make treatment recommendations that are misaligned with FBT principles (e.g., recommending medication or individual treatment where there is no comorbidity).

Supervisory Intervention

When clinicians are early in training, supervisors provide basic didactic training around the medical complications of eating disorders and associated renourishment requirements. For example, a short review of medical complications might proceed as follows:

When an individual has been malnourished, this has many different negative consequences on the physical body. In an effort to survive, the body goes into hibernation mode to help conserve resources. As a result, the body's temperature lowers, causing hypothermia, the heart rate slows to a dangerously low rate, called bradycardia, and there can be significant arrhythmias and changes in blood pressure and heart rate that can lead to dizziness, fainting and, in most severe cases, cardiac arrest. Individuals who are malnourished often feel cold all the time and may develop a growth of hair called lanugo on their body to help keep them warm. Further, for girls, the menstrual cycle often stops due to decreased production of hormones. These hormones are also responsible for supporting bone growth and strength, and without them individuals are at increased risk for osteopenia, and in some cases, eventual osteoporosis, which can lead to bone fractures. We also know that generalized atrophy of the brain occurs in starvation—we see loss of both white and grey matter volumes and elevated levels of cerebral spinal fluid. We can see these changes manifest in real life in problems with cognition: individuals with restrictive eating disorders may struggle with rigid and obsessional thoughts and with working memory. Other consequences may be associated with dehydration, purging using laxatives and or self-induced vomiting, which can cause dangerous shifts in the levels of electrolytes, or salts, in the blood that help regulate cardiac rhythms. When these shifts occur, an individual becomes vulnerable to cardiac arrest. These serious consequences of starvation help explain why AN in particular has the highest mortality rate of any psychiatric disorder (Brown & Mehler, 2015).

The supervisor should assist the clinician in tailoring delivery of this medical feedback to the family as related to their specific concerns and experiences. Not all families coming to treatment may have encountered significant medical consequences firsthand. It is the clinician's job to amplify the presenting concerns of an individual family.

The following vignette reflects some of the challenges highlighted earlier with regards to early treatment engagement. The goal is to assist clinicians in setting an FBT framework with families from the earliest points of contact. In this case, the clinician was early in her training, having no prior eating disorder experience, and had only recently taken her first two FBT cases. She had completed training in FBT and read the manual prior to initiation of supervision.

She was assigned a case from an inpatient eating disorder medical unit—a 16-year-old female with a one-year history of AN. This was her second hospitalization, and the family had previously pursued individual treatment to address poor body image and low mood, with no change in eating behaviors and ongoing significant weight loss. The referral for FBT was placed with the associated outpatient program and the family scheduled the first appointment with the front desk staff within days of the patient's discharge.

In preparation for the first meeting, the clinician had reviewed inpatient progress notes, including a full history and physical. The first session was video-recorded with the family's permission for supervisory purposes.

At the outset of the session, the clinician was perplexed when she found only the mother and daughter in the waiting room. She was aware there was a younger sibling at home and that the patient came from an intact household. She addressed their absence briefly at the beginning of the session, and learned that the father was not present due to work obligations and the family did not know the younger sibling was meant to attend. The clinician then proceeded to begin Session 1, taking a family history and a history of the eating disorder and communicating the gravity of the illness. Halfway through the session, the patient's mother expressed confusion, stating, "I don't understand, I thought this was going to be individual therapy. Do you want me to leave the room?" The clinician admittedly experienced anxiety and confusion around the mother's question and expressed uncertainty about how to respond in supervision, ultimately deciding to acknowledge her lack of awareness of this recommendation and to plan to communicate this question to her supervisor and the team.

Here the primary supervisory dilemma was related to challenges with the orientation to the treatment framework prior to the first session. The clinician was under the erroneous assumption that the family had been well oriented to FBT and was aware of the referral, the procedures and rationale for this recommended approach. In supervision, the supervisor quickly identified primary goals, which were to:

- Assist the clinician in learning orientation strategies to FBT
- To raise common dilemmas clinicians face in orienting families (e.g., referral stream and communication breakdowns)
- To assist the clinician in understanding the rationale for the introductory phone call
- To help the clinician take corrective steps to repair early rupture
- To highlight FBT-specific goals in this initial meeting (engaging the entire family), with the aim of identifying strategies to address barriers

Here, the supervisor said, *One of the important points I think you have learned here is that we cannot assume that families have received clear information about the recommended referral, the rationale for this referral and expectations for follow-up care. In FBT, beginning well starts with an initial phone call to the family. In the future, when you are aware of a new referral, contacting the family directly yourself is an important step in the engagement process. This phone call provides an opportunity to introduce yourself, highlight the expectation that the entire family attend the session, provide a clear rationale for this request, problem-solving any barriers that arise up front, and ensure that the entire family is able to attend prior to scheduling the first session.*

Further, the supervisor helped the clinician troubleshoot potential challenges that might arise in this phone call—namely, responding to barriers to bring the entire family. *In FBT, the goal of the first session is to engage each family member as they have all been impacted directly by AN. You might draw the following analogy for the family—imagine that the nurses on your child's unit had an important meeting scheduled to train them in the refeeding protocol, and one of the primary nurses was left out of this meeting. The impact of her exclusion may be that she is confused and continues to engage in behaviors that contradict the protocol and potentially undermine it. The family session provides an opportunity for everyone in the family who is struggling to support your child get on the same page to ensure that everyone is working together as a team.*

The supervisor also identified the clinician's lack of confidence in responding to the family confusion as a point of intervention (this may not have been as apparent had the supervisor not watched a video recording of the session). Here, the clinician became anxious as would many who are early in their training and faced with a divergence from their plan to follow textbook interventions. The supervisor is interested in not only strengthening general clinical skills but also helping the clinician do so in a way that is consistent with the goal of orienting and engaging the family in FBT. *In this instance, I would pause and not proceed with any intervention until the miscommunication was better understood. Instead of letting the family know you would communicate this with the treatment team and check with your supervisor about the recommendation for individual therapy, I would ask them to repeat what they had been told by the team and their understanding of follow-up recommendations. Further, I would explain my understanding of the recommendation and identify any gaps in their knowledge to correct any misconceptions. Here, families may have preconceived expectations about psychological treatment, and some of this may have been shaped in a way that is counter to FBT theory, even if inadvertently, by other systems and providers. For example, many families enter treatment expecting underlying psychological causes of illness to be the focus of treatment. They may point to supportive relationships their child has had with previous mental health providers (e.g., on an inpatient unit), and be confused by the focus on parents in early stages of FBT.*

Early in supervision, a focus on previewing these challenges in getting families on board is important, as they are likely to arise early in treatment until the family has been properly oriented and strengthened in their commitment to FBT.

Finally, in this case the supervisor would want to address challenges the clinician may encounter with taking an authoritative role, as in this vignette the clinician experienced anxiety around bringing the family back to the FBT model, and became distracted by their interest in alternative treatments.

Supervisor: *Tell me a little bit about the concerns that arose for you in the moment leading to your decision to defer the question of whether individual therapy was recommended to the supervisor.*

Clinician: *I felt I embarrassed that I had launched into the family session without being aware of this concern, and felt the mother's increasing discomfort in the room. I thought that maybe the recommendation had been for individual therapy, and didn't want to act on this until I became clear.*

Supervisor: *What information did you have about what was communicated to the family by other team members prior to starting treatment?*

Clinician: *The referral placed was for family treatment and the discharge plan specified that this had been communicated to the family and they were in agreement.*

Supervisor: *What sorts of concerns and questions arose for you in response to the mother's confusion?*

Clinician: *Well, the mother seemed really worried about her daughter's horrible body image—she said it's been going on since she was really young, even before anorexia started, and that this has been at the root of her depression, so I thought maybe she was right that these needed to be addressed.*

Supervisor: *Ah, I can see why this would feel compelling—as clinicians it is our job to attend to psychological distress and do a thorough assessment of her symptom progression. It is common to be compelled by a family's narrative and belief system about the causes and maintaining features of the eating disorder. However, I want to bring our focus back to the rationale for recommendation of FBT, especially at this stage of her illness. We have limited evidence to suggest that individual treatment is as beneficial as FBT for a wide variety of reasons, which I want to help familiarize you with so you feel confident communicating these to the family. First, due to malnourishment of the brain, cognitive functions are impaired—namely, those that would be required to engage in individual treatment (e.g., abstract reasoning, perspective taking, concentration and attention). Further, AN at its core is an ego-syntonic disease, and as you mentioned this mother is baffled by her daughter's indifference to her life-threatening illness and desire to continue losing weight. These features of the illness make engaging individuals with AN in treatment difficult, as motivation to change is minimal at best. Evidence suggests that addressing behaviors first can lead to subsequent cognitive change. If an individual is fully renourished, yet continues to struggle with these eating disorder cognitions, we will help the family find ways to intervene on this challenge as well.*

Here the supervisor likely recommends readings (see Appendix I) that would help orient the clinician to the features unique to AN that impede progress in individual treatment, and research findings that point to the inclusion of parents in treatment.

As evidenced by this supervision vignette, there are a variety of dilemmas and opportunities for instruction embedded in this discussion. Here, the supervisor chose to focus on helping the clinician set a clear treatment frame and identified barriers to doing so. The primary barriers identified included a lack of information on the clinician's part with regards to treatment rationale, and the important steps involved in setting the therapeutic frame. Further, the supervisor chose to focus on assisting the clinician in building his or her own confidence, modeling language the supervisor could utilize with the family, and also encouraging the clinician to review resources to enhance their understanding of the rationale for these steps.

References

Brown, C., & Mehler, P. S. (2015). Medical complications of anorexia nervosa and their treatments: An update on some critical aspects. *Eating and Weight Disorders, 20*(4), 419–425.

Byrne, C. E., Accurso, E. C., Arnow, K. D., Lock, J., & Le Grange, D. (2015). An exploratory examination of patient and parental self-efficacy as predictors of weight gain in adolescents with anorexia nervosa. *International Journal of Eating Disorders, 48*(7), 883–888.

Forsberg, S., Darcy, A., Bryson, S. W., Arnow, K. D., Datta, N., Le Grange, D., & Lock, J. (2015). Psychological symptoms among parents of adolescents with anorexia nervosa: A descriptive examination of their presence and role in treatment outcome. *Journal of Family Therapy, 39*(4), 514–536.

Katzman, D. K., Peebles, R., Sawyer, S. M., Lock, J., & Le Grange, D. (2013). The role of the pediatrician in family-based treatment for adolescent eating disorders: Opportunities and challenges. *Journal of Adolescent Health, 53*(4), 433–440.

Kyriacou, O., Treasure, J., & Schmidt, U. (2008). Understanding how parents cope with living with someone with anorexia nervosa: Modelling the factors that are associated with carer distress. *International Journal of Eating Disorders, 41*(3), 233–242.

Lock, J., Agras, W. S., Bryson, S., & Kraemer, H. C. (2005). A comparison of short- and long-term family therapy for adolescent anorexia nervosa. *American Academy of Child and Adolescent Psychiatry, 44*(7), 632–639.

Zabala, M. J., Macdonald, P., & Treasure, J. (2009). Appraisal of caregiving burden, expressed emotion and psychological distress in families of people with eating disorders: A systematic review. *European Eating Disorders Review, 17*(5), 338–349.

4 Session 1

*Sarah Forsberg, Kathleen Kara Fitzpatrick,
James Lock and Daniel Le Grange*

Background on Session 1

Clinicians are faced with accomplishing many aims in the first session—they must work to join the family by engaging them, gather relevant history as it relates to the current dilemma of the eating disorder (ED), and orient the family to the structure and rationale for FBT. Further, clinicians balance a focus on content and process, observing the family narrative as it unfolds with systemic questioning designed to assess family organization around the illness. Given the complexity of the first session, and the impact this initial meeting may have on subsequent sessions, helping clinicians to be successful here is critical. We suggest that supervisors and clinicians utilize the treatment fidelity manual (included as an appendix here) as a session-by-session guide. It can be used by the supervisor to assess for the presence of these interventions (adherence), as well as with those who are advancing in their understanding as an opportunity to reflect on evolving competence. Clinicians in training are encouraged to use this instrument to self-assess sessions as a springboard for supervision and identification of questions.

The strategies a supervisor uses will vary according to the developmental stage of the clinician. In preparation for supervision of the first session, you may ask yourself, what strengths and skills does this clinician in training bring, and where do I anticipate he or she may have challenges? To prepare for this discussion, it is helpful to reflect on early assessment of the clinician's background and goals to guide your own thinking about how to structure and focus your supervision time. Common challenges based on training or past experience are described ahead, and should help you prepare for the supervision meeting. Frequent assessment of the clinician's developmental stage is useful throughout supervision of different sessions, and a similar framework applies.

Becoming a Family Therapist: A Developmental Framework

Preparing for the Supervision Session When the Therapist Is New to Family Therapy

In preparing clinicians who have never done family therapy and have not done FBT, they should be encouraged to prepare by reviewing the manual and the specific interventions (see the fidelity instrument). An initial discussion of the arc of the session, how the interventions fit together and build upon one another, and common points of departure with the clinician will also be important, as these nuances are not necessarily contained in a description of each intervention. It can be quite helpful to review a first FBT session with them (or ask them to watch a few on their own), helping them to identify the interventions, while highlighting their timing and integration in the context of the family narrative. If clinicians have no background in family therapy, a primer on the models from which FBT was drawn may further anchor their understanding to a theoretical rationale for the specified interventions (Dare & Eisler, 1997; Minuchin et al., 1975; Palazzoli, 1974).

Review of the Session

In your first supervision after the initial session, with novice FBT clinicians, reviewing an intervention by intervention accounting of the session provides an opportunity to observe where the clinician is challenged, if interventions are left out, and if there are misunderstandings about the theoretical rationale for any of the interventions. Supervisors often will have the opportunity to view "live" sessions, either through a one-way mirror or through recordings. Though this can be time-consuming, it is often worthwhile. If the supervisor has access to video, watching alongside the trainee provides many opportunities to stop and reflect on in-session behavior and the supervisor may pause following delivery of specific interventions to discuss them in greater detail. Without video, the following types of questions will support clinician learning of the rationale behind Session 1 interventions, and enhance the clinician's account of the content of the intervention and session. The supervisor should begin each supervision session as one does in therapy—by setting an agenda. In these early stages the agenda may include an intervention-by-intervention accounting of the session. The supervisor may first ask the clinician to identify his own challenges in conducting the session to assess the clinician's self-reflective capacity in the context of the new model. The following questions may help guide the supervision session, and may also be provided as a framework for clinicians to engage in self-reflection in preparation for the supervision session.

Session 1 Supervisory Guide

- *Tell me about the first greeting—how did you find yourself conveying a sense of gravity in your introduction to the family?*
- *What did you observe about the emotional tenor of the family?*
- *How did people introduce themselves?*
- *Who spoke first?*
- *How did others respond to this individual's perspective?*
- *Walk me through how the family shared the history of the ED.*

- *Were any family narratives discounted or left out/silenced?*
- *Were there conflicting views of the problem and why?*
- *What was the pacing of the session—that is, how much time did you spend on each of the interventions? Did you find yourself getting stuck or rushing through specific interventions?*

You will want to help the clinician organize information about how people are responding and how the family has reorganized itself around the illness—for example, who carries the most worry, how do others respond to this worry, are parents aligned? Are there coalitions or triangulations? What was the lag time between identification of the illness, and what barriers did the family face in pursuing treatment? The kinds of familial patterns that you will help your clinician monitor include:

- *What family dynamics are important inasmuch as they maintain the ED?*
- *To what extent did these arise in the context of the ED how have things changed?*
- *Examples of family dynamics to explore include:*

  - **Coalitions:** *When two members of family form an alliance against a third member.*
  - **Enmeshment:** *Occurs when boundaries between family members are blurred; oftentimes these are intergenerational boundaries. The degree of closeness challenges the development of autonomy.*
  - **Hostility and criticism—self-blame and guilt:** *Families often oscillate between blaming themselves, experiencing significant guilt and blaming others, leading to hostility and outward criticism.*
  - **Inverted family structure:** *Family hierarchy is flipped—parents are disempowered and passive and struggle to set limits, for example.*

In asking these assessment-focused questions, the supervisor is helping clinicians attune to such patterns in future sessions. They reflect the kind of thinking that is consistent with a family model of treatment and may help clinicians anticipate family strengths and challenges. Clinicians can also be taught to reflect on their own response to families—for example, when interventions are left out entirely, or delivered in a way that is not fidelitous to the model, clinicians can be trained to question whether these observations are diagnostic of the family atmosphere.

Of course, in these early stages, new clinicians are already tasked with learning the interventions and the "language" of FBT, which may feel incongruent with previous modes of learning (e.g., especially those that are more psychodynamically oriented or process-oriented). As a result, as a supervisor, you may find yourself frequently reassessing the optimal dosing of your teaching, and the balance may be shifted toward a focus on utilizing symbolic methods (e.g., didactic teaching of interventions, providing sample phrasing and clinical case examples that support adherence to the interventions required).

Becoming an FBT Therapist

Understanding the Difference Between Traditional Family Therapy and FBT

In many cases, seasoned clinicians who have experience in family therapy are interested in learning FBT. There are unique challenges that arise in working to help these clinicians shift the balance of focus to *present-moment* management of symptoms and family patterns inasmuch as they maintain the illness. In many cases, clinicians with previous family therapy training (e.g., in structural or systemic models) are apt to focus on family processes more broadly, the ways in which these serve a *causal* or maintaining role in the eating disorder. This focus is incongruent with FBT in that the approach is *agnostic* and presupposes only that family function has been *disrupted* by the eating disorder, and thus maladaptive patterns result from accommodations the family has made to trying to help their child. Here, you may find it useful to spend time learning about the clinician's view of the eating disorder as formulated by his or her ascribed theoretical orientation. This should occur as early as possible in the supervision relationship, ideally during the assessment period. While the training addresses the agnostic view, it is unlikely for strongly held beliefs about the etiology of eating disorders to diminish in this context. By exploring with your clinician, you will have an opportunity to intervene early (rather than waiting to find out the clinician has had difficulty keeping the FBT framework) in facilitating discussion of the ways in which these conceptualizations may contradict and thus interfere with the effectiveness of FBT. When clinicians have difficulty shifting their orientation, common pitfalls are apt to arise, including:

- *Failure to interrupt unhelpful feelings of shame and guilt associated with parental fears that they have caused their child's illness*
- *Difficulty redirecting focus from causal mechanisms or family processes*
- *Ineffective use of externalization, in the event that the eating disorder is viewed as serving some important function for the individual (e.g., helping the child "regain control," or serving to "get attention" in the context of unmet attachment needs)*

Prior family therapy training most predictably impacts key tenets of FBT—externalization, agnosticism and parental empowerment. Preliminary data suggests that success in FBT may rely on effective use of externalization, parental unity, parental management of ED symptoms and low levels of criticism (Ellison et al., 2012). Thus as a supervisor, your attunement to the ways in which FBT diverges from traditional family therapy models and how to help clinicians in training learn to differentiate FBT from these models is critical.

Review of the Session

In reviewing the session, we encourage supervisors to prompt clinicians to observe their experience of this new form of family therapy with a specific focus on the common challenges (e.g., remaining agnostic, externalizing, decreasing parental blame, parental empowerment). The aim of this supervision approach is to encourage self-monitoring in the session, and facilitate an open dialogue by normalizing the challenges that come with shifting one's conceptualization and approach. When clinicians diverge from FBT, this can be directly observed in the supervision process

Supervision Case Vignette

In supervision with a new FBT clinician, with prior psychodynamic training and a specialty in eating disorders treatment, the supervisor asked the clinician to share the history of AN. The clinician began to describe the behavioral and physical characteristics of the patient, noting the following,

> *She appears to dress like a boy, even her haircut is short, I wonder about the role of gender identity in the context of the patient beginning to enter puberty and develop secondary sex characteristics—it seems that this precipitated the onset of AN and she may have felt compelled to maintain a more masculine physique.*

In this instance, the supervisor paused the clinician, saying,

> *While this may be a compelling narrative, I hear you hypothesizing around cause, which if pursued, will interfere with your ability to remain agnostic and support the family in doing the same.*

From there, the supervisor and clinician explored the factors precipitating the focus on gender identity (e.g., it will be helpful to understand whether this reflects the family narrative, requiring direct intervention on the part of the clinician), the clinician is listening in a way that reflects previous learning around the etiology of AN, in which case the supervisor would problem-solve strategies to remain agnostic and present-symptom-focused in the midst of compelling material that reflects training in other modalities.

The supervisor might also encourage the clinician to reflect on why it is challenging to stay focused on the task at hand—helping parents disrupt behaviors maintaining low weight (e.g., the patient undereating, overexercising or purging). This is the time to reinforce the use of the specific interventions by reviewing the rationale for these interventions, and the impact of pursuing theoretical approaches on the integrity of the treatment.

Expectations for the Advanced FBT Clinician

Preparation for the Supervision Session

For those clinicians who have somewhat more experience with FBT, their preparation for the session may be focused differently. This is a good time for clinicians to reflect on their experience with the model thus far, with a focus on where they feel skilled and fluid in their application of interventions and where they remain challenged. Common difficulties for clinicians in this early stage often surround management of family process and the interweaving and pacing of interventions, rather than their understanding and delivery of the specific interventions. Clinicians may be primed to examine shifts in their practice as an opportunity for exploration of family process that may have important treatment implications (e.g., spending a significant amount of time on externalization in families where there is a high level of blame and difficulty tolerating distress around eating).

Review of the Session

As clinicians gain experience, they should naturally progress in their ability to provide an account of the family session with diminished prompting over time. If you have helped to orient clinicians to the structure of session presentation early in supervision, they should begin to direct their own thinking in a similar way. In instances where this does not occur, you may ask, what is being left out? Where does this individual get stuck and why? What does the clinician not understand about the individual interventions and how they are woven effectively throughout the session? Clinicians with more experience will begin to rely on the structure of the intervention as a method for discovering important information about family process—for example, you will observe clinicians identifying family strengths—how have they been successful in areas outside of management of AN and within? How have they reorganized themselves to accommodate AN, and what is particularly compelling to the family about their child's illness (e.g., are they alarmed by the extent of distress and anxiety experienced by their child, do they wish to respect their child's autonomy, have they had experience in setting firm limits previously?). The challenges clinicians at this stage observe are an opportunity to reflect on their assessment of family features that have a direct impact on their own experience and style in delivering interventions.

Shifting From an Individual to a Family Therapy Focus

Description of Challenge

This is a common dilemma novice clinicians face, as they are much more likely to have experience working with individual patients, where developing a strong therapeutic relationship is foundational. Further, clinicians may be accustomed to efforts to build motivation for treatment as a prerequisite for pursuing change-focused interventions. These efforts to get "buy-in" from patients may both detract from engaging the entire family in the history-gathering process and inadvertently send the message to the family that the child must be equally committed to engage in treatment.

Supervisory Intervention

As a supervisor, you may preview the challenges associated with a focus on parental empowerment and externalization to strengthen parental resolve to take control over weight restoration. Further, you may encourage the clinician to actively work to separate communications arising out of eating disordered beliefs from those that are reflective of a healthy perspective, as it is the clinician's job to differentially respond to model effectiveness for the parents. The clinician may need to learn to redirect and differentially ignore eating disorder behaviors and comments in the session, which can be difficult given the desire to be supportive of the adolescent. If a clinician is able to model these behaviors, parents are much more likely to follow suit.

Actively Engaging the Entire Family

Description of the Dilemma

Active engagement of the family is a skill that may take time to develop for family therapy neophytes. We define active clinicians as those who expand and reframe statements made by the family as a means of introducing new language (e.g., externalization) and highlighting the goals of treatment. They also tie concepts together and amplify important areas of focus, with efforts to use issues or concerns identified by the family to make points in session. This can be considered a "bottom-up" strategy, in which what happens in session or is described by the family is used to illustrate a concept and then generalized for the family. It is important to note that active clinicians are not prescriptive ("You should feed her more butter"), but rather make observations drawing from material in session ("It sounds like AN gets more activated when you butter the toast"). Active clinicians can jump in and redirect the focus of treatment, both directly ("I'm curious about something you just said, can we go back to that for a minute?"), as well as indirectly by the questions they choose to ask, the emotions they want to amplify and the events and issues that they spend time on in session. An active clinician is one who understands the integrated nature of many of the techniques used in FBT and pays attention to timing in sessions to introduce or expand these concepts. Practicing the skills we want families to use while they are in session is the best way we can teach and guide use of these skills. Active clinicians are also adept at tolerating or managing emotions in the session, providing empathy or context for the challenges of renourishment rather than attempting to alleviate this distress. For example, reminding parents that the challenges they face in helping their child eat more are excellent examples of why they need to step in, as their child would not be able to manage these difficulties on his or her own. At other times, active clinicians can also preempt concerns. For example, when sharing the weight, stating that the type of weight gain is *"healthy and expected, exactly on target with our expectations"* or by initiating a conversation about agnosticism by saying something such as, *"We do not know what causes AN, just the way we do not know what causes most cancers, but that does not mean we do not treat both diseases aggressively and with treatments that we know to be effective in eliminating these diseases."*

Typically, as clinicians are getting started in a family model, and FBT specifically, they understandably will not be adept in utilizing these more advanced skills, and alternatively may proceed in a more "by-the-book" manner. You may experience novice FBT clinicians using their own language without shaping the language of the family. For example, in their own speech they may refer to "AN" or "ED" but when the family describes behaviors that could be externalized this way, the clinician does not actively reshape their language to support separation of the ED from the young person. They may also introduce a concept passively, as though checking a box that this is something they should introduce, without waiting for or expanding upon statements made by the family. For example, an active clinician might utilize the family narrative as a launching point for orchestrating an intense scene—they may note a moment of parental anxiety and distress from which to expand upon, saying, "*As you are describing the experience of watching your son waste away before your eyes I see how incredibly frightened you all feel for him. You are right to worry for him. You took him to the hospital because of your worry and got him help before his health deteriorated further.*" From there, the clinician might highlight and expand upon what the family had learned about the serious health risks of AN while their son was hospitalized.

A challenge for novice clinicians is a tendency to be uncertain about when to guide a conversation that is off-topic or to interrupt a family member who may be moving the session in a direction that distracts from the focus of the session. In addition, they may never provide examples from the family concept to illustrate a point. Often this gives the entire session a fractured feel or as though there are many topics being run through without tying each of these back to efforts toward renourishment. More passive clinicians may nod encouragement for behaviors they see parents engaging in that are appropriate but do not provide direct feedback, like, *That sounds like an excellent way of managing that situation—what happened next?* or problem-solving with parents.

Supervisory Intervention

As a supervisor, you are in the business of shaping not only adherence to the manual but also flexibility within this structure to respond appropriately to family differences as a way of bringing the treatment to life. Given these stylistic variables are much harder to teach and involve significant modeling and practice, this is a place where observation of the clinician is key and will provide rich opportunities for feedback. In the event that supervisors are not able to review audio or videotapes, or join the session through a one-way mirror, for example, they may ask the trainee to demonstrate how he or she utilized family data to teach a concept.

The Art of Circular Questions

Description of the Dilemma

Circular questioning is an important technique used in FBT because family behaviors do not occur in isolation. This type of interviewing stimulates an increased understanding by the family as whole about how familial patterns around the ED arose. For those with no formal systemic family therapy training, this kind of questioning may be difficult to grasp at first, given the complexity of collecting information on family process and interrelated family perspectives. Circular questioning helps us learn about (1) the family narrative around the eating disorder, (2) the sequencing of transactions between family members relating to the emergence of the eating disorder, and (3) how relationships have evolved/changed in the context of the eating disorder.

Supervisory Intervention

In this context, direct practice is most helpful to increase comfort with circular questions. Practice can occur in multiple forms. In preparation for the first session, the supervisor may ask clinicians to generate a list of assessment questions they might use to take the family history and history of the ED. Specific examples may also help guide the new clinician:

- *When did you first notice a change in his or her eating patterns?*
- *At what point did you become concerned enough to take action?*
- *What sorts of changes in her did you notice? How has her eating disorder interfered with her schoolwork, friend relationships and interests?*

General principles of circular questions can be found in an article that is required reading for new trainees in our clinic (Fleuridas, Nelson, & Rosenthal, 1986). These include not focusing for too long on any one family member, and asking questions that directly support hypothesis testing. Following generation of such a list, the supervisor will help the clinician restate these questions to make them circular. Examples of how to make questions circular are as follows:

- From: *When did you notice a change in your daughter's eating?*

  To: *Who in your family was the first to notice a change in his or her eating?*

- From: *What about you, father, do you agree?*

  To: *Who else agrees with this timeline?*

- From: *What do you think, brother?*

  To: *Does anyone see this differently?*

- From: *How did you respond when you first became concerned?*

  To: *How did others in the family know when your father/husband became concerned?*

- From: *How did you try to help her eat more?*

  To: *What do people do when she refuses food?*

The clinician may also share commonly utilized circular questions. The challenge here is to help the clinician maintain this circularity in service of understanding familial relationships. When supervision occurs in a group context, clinicians can take on the role of family members and take turns practicing circular questioning with one another. The goal is to help clinicians complete a circle, carrying questioning to the point of confidence in the original hypothesis.

Remaining Agnostic: Clinician Is Distracted by Causal Discussion

Description of the Dilemma

For clinicians to remain agnostic, they not only refrain from assuming a cause but also actively redirect parents away from exploring causal theories and back toward current renourishment efforts. For many clinicians new to FBT this can be challenging, especially for those who have received training in other therapeutic modalities like psychodynamic, cognitive and Rogerian therapies, for example.

Redirecting the family can take many forms: reminding them that they were successful in nourishing their ill child/other children in the family until the illness appeared as well as reshaping specific statements made by the patient or the parents. Efforts can also be preemptive: *We do not know the cause of this illness, though we know many factors can contribute.* Again the goal is to help clinicians be *active* in this agnostic stance—simply ignoring causal statements made by family members is not sufficient. The clinician will need to identify where the family appears to become stuck: *It sounds like you might be worried that you do not know what your daughter needs, but remember, parents do not cause this illness and you have many skills.* Agnosticism is particularly important as it is meant to support parental empowerment through reducing blame parents may place on themselves and/or their child.

Supervisory Intervention

As a part of your early assessment of clinicians' background, training and goals related to their training in eating disorders, you will have some knowledge of their view on eating disorders and their treatment. If this is not clear, as a supervisor you can begin to ask clinicians about their perspectives—for example, "What sorts of causal mechanisms for eating disorders have you heard? What causal explanations are you likely to face in your conversations with families and other providers?" We find it helpful to give space for eliciting and processing these viewpoints, which are often very compelling, interesting and reflective of the kind of analytical line of inquiry one who finds him- or herself pursuing a career in psychotherapy is drawn to. If there is no discussion of these views during the early stage of supervision, inevitably for those who are novice FBT clinicians, they will arise in the context of treatment, at times with significant consequences to the therapeutic context. This provides a nice opportunity for clinicians to self-reflect and develop a plan for managing their own interests and biases before entering the first session. Further, supervisors may share their own experience with holding causal theories of EDs, and how they have managed to put these aside in delivering FBT. It is not problematic as such to have these in mind; however, introducing them, even inadvertently, can significantly interfere with the focus and success of treatment. The supervisor might highlight the kinds of comments one is likely to hear from families (which generally mirror pervasive beliefs about eating disorders—for example, that they arise out of parental psychopathology, that they are a response to sociocultural pressures and internalization of the thin ideal).

Further, parents and novice clinicians alike often become confused about the directionality of symptom expression, which often arises when there is significant emotion dysregulation, new oppositional behaviors and suicidal ideation, for example. Families often believe that treating these behaviors and underlying distress will result in alleviation of eating symptoms, whereas it is the clinician's job to help them understand the reverse is in fact true (in the vast majority of cases). Early discussions with clinicians about these common challenges are important so they may anticipate such challenges and not be overcome, as families often are, by significant expression of emotional distress, which can derail focus on management of eating symptoms.

Managing Family Criticism

Description of the Dilemma

Efforts here should be active—directly shaping critical comments and behaviors; reframing, restating or redirecting these statements helps manage criticism. There are several clinician interventions that may be helpful here: developing skills in selective ignoring (not attending to or responding to behaviors that distract from the task at hand or redirect the session), helping parents manage their frustration or upset (e.g., teaching specific skills in managing their own distress at these statements or reframing them—most often this is done when efforts at avoiding nourishment result in personal attacks on parents) and helping the family as a whole identify ED behaviors.

Supervisory Intervention

In Session 1 criticism is largely managed through psychoeducation and externalization. Efforts may be subtler, as the clinician may not know the family very well or may be evaluating statements in the context of family communication. Generally speaking, however, criticism in Session 1 should mostly be managed by redirecting family concerns by helping them understand the disorder. This may also include externalization techniques/ the language of externalization, when these are used in direct response to criticism. In supervision, reviewing critical comments/behaviors and modeling specific language to use in response to these are important. The manner in which clinicians respond to criticism has the potential to either defuse/neutralize or create additional tension and defensiveness. Thus, role-playing these discussions in supervision can be a quite helpful practice for clinicians as they enter into tense and oftentimes painful territory with families. In addition, the Venn diagram is a tool commonly used to externalize the illness—bringing to life the ways in which the young person has been coopted by the ED. Supervision is an excellent venue to practice drawing this diagram via a role-play (two overlapping circles highlighting characteristics/qualities of the individual, the ED [e.g., new behaviors that have emerged] and their overlap [often positive traits that are now serving the ED, like determination, focus on detail, and perfectionism]). When utilized effectively, the entire family walks away from this exercise aware that it is the illness that drives maladaptive behaviors, not their child.

Engaging Siblings in a Supportive Role

Description of the Dilemma

Families often express reluctance about bringing siblings into the family treatment. There are many practical barriers families face, yet the clinician must remain committed to the inclusion of siblings and able to provide a strong rationale when families waver.

Supervisory Intervention

Here, clinicians themselves may benefit from a reminder of the rationale for inclusion of siblings so they may communicate this directly to families. Oftentimes, this concern arises even before the initial meeting, and can be discussed with parents in preparation for the first session. Challenges that arise around including siblings can be discussed—these are often based on the age/developmental obstacles to engagement as well as sibling relationships that both predated and developed in response to the eating disorder. Further, parents often want to protect siblings or the adolescent with the eating disorder. Siblings of all ages are impacted by the eating disorder, and may express their concern in various ways. The goal of inclusion is to help siblings understand what their brother or sister is going through and the ways in which each family member can be supportive. We remind parents that when siblings are excluded, they often feel isolated, confused and may engage in unhelpful behaviors that unintentionally interfere with the treatment.

Timing and Pacing of the Session

Description of the Dilemma

In many cases, the clinician spends a largely disproportionate amount of the session gathering history. This is quite common given the tendency to spend more time on assessment in other treatment models. In FBT, the assessment is active and informs strategic generation of movement toward other important interventions (e.g., externalization, agnosticism and orchestration of the intense scene). Thus, clinicians need to be actively listening and shaping family discussion toward these key interventions.

Supervisory Intervention

Most simply, as a supervisor, you can help clinicians plan ahead for the challenge of fitting many interventions into an hour session. You might help them think about these transitions and approximate amounts of time to be spent on each intervention. For example, typically, the first half of the session would include efforts to get to know the family (taking a family history), and a history of AN. Within this, clinicians will be coached to look for opportunities to utilize other interventions, as oftentimes this is where opportunities for agnosticism and externalization arise. The clinician will likely observe in the family narrative the ways in which the individual with the eating disorder has changed (an opportunity to separate the illness: "*You can see how she is no longer herself—you are saying the things she loves most no longer seem as important as losing weight*"). Supervision will also focus on helping the clinician pick out important language that implies a causal mechanism that needs reshaping through direct statements of agnosticism, or feelings of guilt around having caused the illness, requiring clinician efforts to empower parents (e.g., by identifying the key role parents play in recovery, focusing on what they can do to resolve the challenges they face). The second half of the session involves additional psychoeducation about the various physical, psychological and social consequences that arise in the context of eating disorders to mobilize parents to action. After the session has occurred, reviewing a videotape of the session is likely to provide the best information about where the flow halts and starts in order to identify ways of linking interventions, redirecting families and generating movement. The following loose guidelines around time spent on each of these interventions may be useful especially to new FBT clinicians:

- Greeting and orientation to FBT: 10 minutes
- Gathering family history with focus on history of AN using circular questioning: 15–20 minutes
- Externalizing the eating disorder: 5–7 minutes
- Orchestrating the intense scene: 5–7 minutes
- Charging the family with the task of refeeding and summary of session: 10 minutes

Mobilizing Families in Light of the Crisis of the ED: The Clinician is Either Too Light or Too Grave

Description of the Dilemma

Mobilizing the family around the crisis of AN may feel uncomfortable and awkward for individuals new to this approach, as clinicians may feel more naturally inclined to help put families at ease. In attempting to emphasize the seriousness of the illness, some clinicians may use such a grave manner so as to miss the opportunity to instill hope and bring anxiety around the illness to a level that does not immobilize families. In some families, anxiety may already be quite high and the orchestration may not reach the "fever pitch" necessary to engage other families. Additionally, families who have quite a bit of information about the illness may require only reiteration of points, rather than a longer, more detailed description. Ultimately, the critical point of this intervention is to heighten parental drive to engage in the renourishment process and you will work to help clinicians assess their effectiveness around this aim.

Supervisory Intervention

Early on, supervisors may get a "read" on the affective range of clinicians—how they present in supervision in discussing cases may shed light on their interpersonal style. It can be helpful to normalize feelings of discomfort that may arise in presenting an air of gravitas, where the default comfortable response is to join families with humor, chitchat and a desire to spend more time in the getting-to-know-you phase of treatment. Some clinicians do not feel comfortable in an authoritative role, whether it be due to their own history, cultural background, training experiences or comfort with the model. Clinicians may need help achieving the balance between warmth, genuine interest and seriousness in the face of the life-threatening nature of EDs. This is an opportunity for supervisors to model this tone through enactment of the intense scene, highlighting key points the clinician may focus on with families.

Summarizing the Session: Catalyzing Family Action

Description of the Dilemma

It is important to assess family learning and internalization of the goals and tasks of therapy. As such, at the end of the session the clinician engages the family in a review of topics covered and action items for the upcoming week. Problems with time management (e.g., trying to cover too much, not leaving enough time at the end of the session for wrap-up) often interfere with this important process. If clinicians do not incorporate this important review of the main aspects of the session as they relate to between-session work, they lose the opportunity to understand potential barriers to family comprehension and action. When identified earlier, the clinician can assist the family in problem solving around potential challenges. A very specific example might include having a family note-taker, who records areas of focus for the week ahead.

Supervisory Intervention

Supervision provides an opportunity to mirror the structure of therapy sessions. As such, the supervisor saves time (approximately 10 minutes) at the end of supervision to assess the clinician's learning and understanding of next steps. Here, the supervisor emphasizes the importance of this process as it applies to the family therapy session. Some useful questions to ask at the end of therapy/supervision include:

- What are the biggest stuck points we identified this week?
- What is your understanding of your current challenges with regards to overcoming these in the week ahead?
- What solutions did we generate today to address these?
- Can you summarize the steps you plan to take in the upcoming week(s) to apply these solutions?

From here, the supervisor has the opportunity to identify any miscommunication that may have occurred, and further explore incongruence between the intended intervention and its interpretation. When information is not internalized as intended, the supervisor hypothesizes about potential causes. Common barriers in both supervision and in family therapy include:

- Learning differences: Explore how individuals best learn and encode information. What strategies are most effective (may refer back to different modes of supervision)?
- Internal dialogue and narratives: Consider whether the individual is struggling to shift his or her preexisting narratives to be more aligned with the current intervention. For families, these narratives may relate to expectations about therapy, stigma and bias with regards to mental health.
- Cultural norms, backgrounds and differences in language: Do these areas need further exploration?
- Emotional distress: Consider verbal and nonverbal cues to individuals' emotional states. Identify and address these to the extent that they are interfering with higher-order cognition.

Fidelity Coding Framework

The fidelity instrument was developed for the purpose of coding FBT therapy sessions for fidelity and assessing and examining its relationship to treatment outcome (Fitzpatrick et al., 2015; Forsberg et al., 2015). Thus, these codes are meant to be examples and when rating across an entire session may encompass different degrees of fidelity at different time points. The fidelity instrument has been developed and explored only for Session 1 and 2 and the remainder of Phase I. Benchmarks for key interventions associated with Phase II and III have yet to be developed. The fidelity instrument may serve multiple purposes:

- Help clinicians prepare and guide them during the session to ensure nothing is left out.

- Assist both the supervisor and clinician in supervision to structure the discussion.
- For advanced clinicians, it may serve as a guide to monitor progress and allow for self-reflection. For example, you can utilize this to encourage anticipation of challenges based on training background and personal style, problem-solve around common challenges (e.g., the clinician finds themselves attracted to causal discussion, or is uncertain about how to invite siblings to participate in a supportive role) and evaluate progression in learning.

A full copy of the fidelity coding framework can be found in Appendix V. Benchmarks for interventions in Session 1 include:

- Greeting the family in a sincere and grave manner
- Engaging each family member in information gathering
- Taking a history of the eating disorder
- Externalizing the illness
- Orchestrating an intense scene
- Reducing guilt and blame
- Remaining agnostic
- Modifying criticism
- Charging the parents with the task of refeeding

References

Dare, C., & Eisler, I. (1997). Family therapy for anorexia nervosa. In D. Garner & P. Garfinkel (Eds.), *Handbook of treatment for eating disorders* (2nd ed., pp. 307–324). New York: Guilford Press.

Ellison, R., Rhodes, P., Madden, S., Miskovic, J., Wallis, A., Baillie, A., . . . Touyz, S. (2012). Do the components of manualized family-based treatment for anorexia nervosa predict weight gain? *International Journal of Eating Disorders, 45*(4), 609–614.

Fitzpatrick, K. K., Accurso, E. C., Aspen, V., Forsberg, S. E., Le Grange, D., & Lock, J. (2015). Conceptualizing fidelity in FBT as the field moves forward: How we know when we're doing it right? In K. L. Loeb, D. Le Grange, & J. Lock (Eds.), *Family therapy for adolescent eating and weight disorders: New applications* (pp. 418–439). New York: Routledge.

Fleuridas, C., Nelson, T. S., & Rosenthal, D. M. (1986). The evolution of circular questions: Training family therapists. *Journal of Marital and Family Therapy, 12*(2), 113–127.

Forsberg, S., Fitzpatrick, K. K., Darcy, A., Aspen, V., Accurso, E. C., Bryson, S. W., . . . Lock, J. (2015). Development and evaluation of a treatment fidelity instrument for family-based treatment of adolescent anorexia nervosa. *International Journal of Eating Disorders, 48*(1), 91–99.

Minuchin, S., Baker, L., Rosman, B., Liebman, R., Milman, L., & Todd, T. (1975). A conceptual model of psychosomatic illness in children. *Archives of General Psychiatry, 32*(8), 1031–1038.

Palazzoli, S. M. (1974). *Self-starvation: From the intrapsychic to the transpersonal approach.* Oxford, UK: Chaucer.

5 Session 2

Sarah Forsberg, Kathleen Kara Fitzpatrick, James Lock and Daniel Le Grange

Background on Session 2

The focus in Session 2 is on renourishment efforts, with the goal being to utilize the family meal itself to promote these efforts. Session 2 is the most behaviorally active and directive session for the clinician, who can and should provide more specific guidance for parental behavior and actively work to shape skills and problem solving. As such, greater direction can be provided in these sessions and using specific examples from the family's experiences is essential. For many clinicians, the family meal session provokes a sense of anxiety and discomfort that is often mirrored in the family's response when they hear that they will be eating in front of the clinician. In the session, the clinician is tasked with both observing family process—the who, what, where, when and why of all aspects of the meal, from planning, preparation and serving to mealtime intervention—and modeling more effective refeeding efforts.

When thinking about this session, it can be useful to think about clinicians who approach these tasks in a "bottom-up" versus a "top-down" process. In "bottom-up" the clinician uses materials, examples and even food items that are present in the session to reinforce a point, and then helps the family generalize these. The use of these concrete and specific examples from session, or family report, is often the easiest for families to understand and to use to expand. In contrast, when clinicians use more general statements and do not integrate these into the learning within the session, they miss the opportunity to help a family learn more efficiently. In preparing clinicians for the family meal session, their developmental level will impact the extent to which they are able to flexibly move between information gathering and directing family process and change.

The interventions delivered in Session 2 include the following:

- Weighing the patient
- Gathering a family history of food preparation and mealtime patterns
- Observing family process, specifically as it relates to interactions around eating with the adolescent

- Assisting parents in helping their child to eat more than he or she has planned, *and/or* supporting parents in working together to help their child gain weight
- Aligning siblings in a supportive role
- Summarizing the session

Preparation for the Session

The family meal session is unusual in that unless clinicians have spent a significant amount of time in more intensive treatment programs (e.g., an inpatient medical unit), they are unlikely to have viewed the personal rituals of a family, or an eating disorder (ED) for that matter, in such a direct fashion. Families too are often perplexed by the notion of eating a meal with the clinician watching, and frequently offer to prepare extra for the clinician. In anticipation of the session, especially for neophyte clinicians, you may preview the common feelings the meal session is likely to evoke. It is quite normal for a clinician to feel a sense of unease or discomfort, often a mirror to the family's own response. Families may feel on the spot and uncertain about the purpose of the meal, and are often already quite stressed during mealtimes. It is helpful for the clinician to normalize this for the family; thus the parallel process of previewing these challenges that you initiate in supervision will likely support the clinician in working most effectively with the family.

We find that for many who are new to FBT, being able to observe a family meal session either in person (through a one-way mirror, or sitting in the session) or on video can be very helpful and dispel some of the concerns many clinicians have. For example, common questions at this early stage include: What happens if the family doesn't bring a meal? What do I do if the child refuses to eat at all? What if everything goes well—how do I intervene? Do kids ever throw food? What if the child runs out of the office? There is limited information on what actually occurs in family meal sessions, making them ever more mysterious. Case presentations of meal sessions often depict the most average case—the child struggles to eat in some way, the eating disorder is evoked in the session, and the clinician is able to successfully coach the parents to get "one bite more" in. While this is the ideal session, and often more typical, the diversity of situations that may arise can lead to anxious anticipation on the part of the clinician. The aim in supervision is to help the clinician understand the structure of the session, utilizing this structure to frame difficult behaviors while sending parents off empowered with new skills to manage eating disorder behaviors. Thus, the supervisor can help to frame this session as an opportunity for learning on the part of both the clinician and family, and frame challenges (e.g., being unable to get the child to eat) as opportunities to support learning (in this instance, parents learn about eating disorder strategies to thwart parental efforts). In this way, as a supervisor you are shoring up the clinician to weather the storm and keep parental empowerment and problem solving intact even in the midst of their distress.

Further, emphasizing the pacing of the session may also be helpful. For example, the clinician will need to learn to balance verbal information gathering with behavioral observations. Questions should be direct and targeted to determine the extent to which the meal unfolding in session is consistent with meal structure at home (and the ways in which families have modified typical patterns in response to the eating disorder). Clinicians are also tasked with helping families observe eating disorder behaviors with the aim of separating these from the adolescent to support appropriate limit setting and decrease accommodation of the eating disorder. Further, they provide information where needed—where parents are limited in their knowledge base, particularly about appropriate nutrition, clinicians should be comfortable with the basic principles of renourishment in ED (i.e., "nutrition 101"). Specifically, clinicians provide a context—they note that these adolescents often need more than their siblings, more than their parents and need more than they were eating before the illness developed. Reminding parents of the goal of weight gain—typically 1–2 pounds per week initially—and the importance of early weight gain in recovery reinforces the learning process.

In addition to orienting the new clinician to the nutritional needs, you will also want to help the clinician attune to the need for both overt data collection through verbal assessment and behavioral observation of family patterns. It is important for the supervisor to highlight common familial patterns early on in supervision. Here again, the aim is to help parents with renourishment efforts and to quickly identify behaviors that accommodate the illness, or those that will undermine parental efforts. Ahead we discuss supervision strategies to support these observations.

Common Dilemmas

Gathering a Thorough Understanding of Family Mealtimes (the Who, Where, When, What and How)

Description of Challenge

How the clinician obtains the history is important and this intervention is a good example of a place where a "bottom-up" strategy may be most beneficial. The goals here are to understand the specifics of what a family brought for the current meal: who selected the meal, observations of how they serve it and what/how much is served to each family member, caloric density of the meal and how typical this meal is for the family in general. By the end of the session, the clinician should have a solid idea of the way meals go in this family and where there are obstacles to renourishment, and have an understanding of the ways these issues may contribute to maintaining (or overcoming) the illness. It should be noted that gathering this information does not mean that the clinician needs to act on it (doing so would certainly require a much longer session)—only that this is the information that should be gathered here for future intervention.

Supervisory Intervention

In helping new clinicians prepare for the session, you can review the questions they will need to ask to ascertain additional details about the family mealtime structure and process. It is important to provide families with space to begin the process of serving and eating the meal, while interspersing questions to enhance their understanding of behaviors as they unfold. The following are key questions to be reviewed in advance in preparation for the session:

- *How did you decide upon what to bring today?*
- *How does this meal compare to what you would typically have at home?*
- *Who is responsible for which elements of meal planning (planning, shopping, preparing, portioning)?*
- *How has the structure and process of meals changed with the development of the eating disorder?*

You will also want to prime the clinician to attend to the ways in which the family has begun to accommodate the eating disorder, and the kinds of patterns that are likely to obstruct or support the renourishment process. For novice clinicians, review these questions in advance of the session and in the supervision following the meal.

- Where do people sit? Who is close with whom? Are there any structural issues that could impact parents supporting the ill adolescent (e.g., a parent who is seated at the far end of the table from the patient, and is attending to his or her own meal or siblings' meals). This is important in that the goal is to physically structure the family to support parental alignment and attunement to the task at hand, while minimizing interruption of this process by siblings in positioning them in a supportive role.
- How is the meal served? Who chooses the portion? Do parents agree on portion sizes? The goal is to understand who is empowered and in the role of choosing and serving meals, and whether the child with the eating disorder has any involvement in this process. When this is the case, the clinician will want to quickly intervene to position parents in an authoritative role, reminding them of the importance of taking responsibility for all aspects of renourishment. When one parent chooses the meal and portions the meal, it is important to inquire about the "behind the scenes" conversation surrounding the task to *work together* to identify a meal that they believe provides the proper nourishment. If it is clear that one parent has taken full responsibility, the clinician intentionally asks the other parent to comment on the choice: "What would you serve your child?" "Is there anything you might change about the portion size?"
- How does the child with the ED respond to the structure? Does the child begin eating unprompted? What food does the child start with?

Does the child get up from the table? Begin to cry or shout? How do others in the family respond to these behaviors? It is rare for there to be no resistance, although this does happen. However, in most instances, clinicians will observe the ways families respond and thus identify areas for teaching and problem solving with the family.

- Review of the session: Given the importance of understanding family mealtime patterns and barriers to the refeeding process, typically, regardless of the developmental level of the clinician, it is useful to review the specific details of typical mealtime patterns and their manifestation in the session. The foregoing questions may be utilized in the review of the session as well.

When the Eating Disorder Escalates: Management of Aggressive Behaviors and Emotional Dysregulation

Description of the Dilemma

When the eating disorder is confronted directly, as it is in the family meal, the goal is to in fact bring it out into the open, so to speak. This is often confusing for families, who may feel as though by pushing their child to eat, they are inflicting emotional pain. It is important for clinicians to model tolerance of emotional distress and compassion for the child who suffers at the hands of the ED, in order to effectively teach parents to stay the course in these moments. The ED may manifest its resistance in many forms, including a quiet hardening against parental efforts (stiff body language, a vacant cool stare), outright defiance (yelling, crossing their arms, getting up from the table, at times getting physical, shouting profanities), melting in a puddle of tears and helplessness, or with heightened emotional lability that is unresponsive to any soothing or intervention. In the family meal (and in all meals in the home), these outward manifestations of distress can be quite effective in getting parents to step back. Clinicians thus need to be adept at tolerating these kinds of behaviors themselves, normalizing them in the context of the aim of confronting the eating disorder, and need to have a range of skills to respond effectively. For most novice clinicians, these moments can be anxiety-provoking and leave them stumped. In these instances, the risk is both that parents will lose faith in the consultation skills of the clinician and parents themselves will feel compelled to do the opposite of what is being asked—that is, searching for strategies to minimize distress (often outsourcing to individual clinicians)—and pull back in their efforts to refeed.

Supervisory Intervention

PREPARATION FOR THE SESSION

Just as clinicians must help prepare families (as best they can) for the common challenges that arise in the refeeding process, so too can supervisors help prepare clinicians. To illustrate, the supervisor may review these in advance of the session in order to model the kind of language clinicians often provide families, as well as to practice problem solving in planning ahead. Supervisors therefore should:

- Remind clinicians that the goal of the session is to engage the eating disorder: *When we bring the eating disorder into the room, we are able to fight it rather than leaving the child to struggle internally on his own* and that compliance does not mean that the patient eats with no struggle.
- Teach basic principles of behaviorism: *There may be extinction bursts when we dare to set new limits and we can use obvious analogies to help parents understand the need to persist—for example, that of a toddler being told he or she may not have a candy bar in the grocery checkout line.*
- Focus on the goal of helping parents to separate the distress that the illness is causing their child from their own distress in order to be effective.
- Emphasize strategies to help parents to create a sense of containment for their child—a safe environment for all family members—and this means having structures in place to manage safety concerns, creating firm consequences for unsafe behavior.
- Review principles of authoritative parenting to help parents in learning to balance warmth and firmness when setting limits. Parents can draw on previous skills in thinking about how they might apply these strategies to management of the eating disorder.
- In reviewing these principles, the supervisor may encourage those clinicians who have not had significant training in childhood development, management of emotion dysregulation and crisis intervention to seek out additional resources. For example, watching meals is the best way to learn about the kinds of skills needed in the types of challenging moments that are likely to arise. Observing other clinicians effectively model these skills may help decrease the likelihood of clinicians becoming anxious when confronting these conflicts in session and thus inadvertently colluding with the family in avoidance (e.g., they may agree with parents when they say the child may stop eating so as to stop the child's screaming). Taking breaks may be important, while reminding clinicians that this is in fact a strategy, as long as it is clearly communicated that the break does not preclude proximal efforts to complete the meal or supplement as needed.

REVIEW OF THE SESSION

Once the session has occurred, the supervisor will be looking for indicators that the ED influenced parents (and possibly the clinician) in their decision making. Thus, the supervisor may ask directly (with the aim of strengthening externalization) for the clinician to describe the ways the ED may have attempted to subvert parental efforts. More experienced clinicians will bring this material directly, identifying the unique challenges they faced in comparison to other families they have worked with, whereas early clinicians will often identify feelings of anxiety or uncertainty around their ability to empower parents in these moments. For new clinicians, the supervisor may share his or her own personal experiences, providing examples of effective interventions in moments of heightened distress or crisis. For more advanced clinicians, you may ask them to reflect on the outcomes of their interventions, and how they might have modified based on their evaluation of barriers to effectiveness.

When an Adolescent Does Not Eat, Will Not Eat "One Bite More"

Description of the Dilemma

Many clinicians express initial concern when learning FBT about what to do in the event that the child refuses to eat. When this occurs, the clinician may use this as an opportunity to externalize the illness, observe the strength of the eating disorder and praise parents for their efforts to try new strategies to refeed their child. How the family and clinician respond to this challenge is of utmost importance—the clinician will need to maintain confidence in the parents' ability to continue to work on the problem outside of the session and convey this directly to the family. The clinician models an important message: *We will just continue the work at home, using the same strategies identified in the session, and catch up with the next meal, and the next.*

Supervisory Intervention

Here it is very important for the supervisor to model confidence in the treatment and in parental abilities for the clinician. Families and treatment providers alike may easily fall into the trap of believing parents will not be able to successfully refeed their child, either through some weakness of their own or a sense that the child's illness is too severe. Supervisors may provide historical examples (especially when clinicians' sample size is quite small and they have not had the variety of cases allowing for reflection on the trouble with predicting outcome at these early stages). A common pitfall for new clinicians is that they may become vulnerable to feelings of hopelessness, given the real sense of urgency around food refusal. New clinicians may benefit from a discussion of the practical strategies to manage medical risk, while continuing to instill a sense of urgency in parental decision making and containment of eating disorder behaviors. For example, you might remind clinicians to encourage families to access medical support in the event their child refuses food for successive meals (24 hours without eating or drinking anything). It is important for supervisors to remind clinicians that learning how to manage these behaviors is also an opportunity to bolster parental resources as parents can practice the skill of effectively utilizing their treatment team and problem solving around these crises.

In reviewing the session it would be unusual for this dilemma not to be the first thing a clinician brings to supervision to discuss following a meal, as it often is perceived as a treatment failure given the focus on getting in "one bite more." Much as the family is tasked with moving forward from this experience with new ideas and a commitment to persist, the supervisor will want to encourage the clinician to reflect on his or her learning from the experience. Thus, the focus will be on the questions, how did the parents respond to their child's refusal, what new skills did they try, and where do they need to focus their efforts moving forward? Clinicians may reflect on what they would have liked to do differently—perhaps they would have structured the room differently, requested that parents sit on either side of the patient, or redirected parents more firmly to the task at hand in the event they became distracted. The idea is to help the clinician integrate data from this experience into their hypotheses about the family and the kinds of interventions that will be key when entering the remainder of Phase I.

The Adolescent Eats "Too" Well—Using Paradoxical Interventions

Description of the Dilemma

Although this appears to be fairly straightforward, it can be challenging if the patient eats easily. The goal is one bite more than the patient intended, and in the case of relative ease of eating, clinician adherence to the therapy involves use of paradoxical interventions. This can involve urging the adolescent to do as the eating disorder requests, reflecting that his or her behavior does not accurately convey what may be happening internally. Further, it can also involve increasing the challenge by asking parents to add to the meal. In rare cases when there is not sufficient food to help a patient eat one more mouthful, the clinician can use hypothetical examples.

Supervisory Intervention

It is often helpful to clarify for the clinician the range of paradoxical injunctions that can be made in response to ease of eating. The common misconception is that the classical injunction of "asking them to eat only if they want to, or do as the eating disorder instructs" is the only way to invite the struggle of the eating disorder into the room. Alternate paradoxical injunctions include pointing out the challenging aspects of their meal ("It is so good to see you eating something like cheese, that is a great calorie-dense food with fats and protein"), or highlighting the likelihood that if the eating disorder had a choice, it would likely not be eating such a meal given its role in restoring weight. If necessary, clinicians can help parents by asking them how this meal is the same as or different from meals at home and help them create a meal that is more similar to what happens at home (in emotional tenor), or perhaps by plating more if they believe that this would be of benefit in the renourishment process. Generally, when the adolescent eats with ease, the clinician breathes a sigh of relief, and as a supervisor you will want to observe this in session and correct the misconception that this is predictive of future behavior, highlighting the importance of parental learning, even in this context.

Assessing the Nutritional Needs of the Child

Description of the Dilemma

The focus of this intervention should be on assisting parents in understanding the need for increased frequency of meals, increased portions and/or increased caloric density. For some families this may also include specific guidance on adding back in foods that are avoided, although this is not always necessary. This is another area in which a bottom-up strategy can be the most effective, using items brought to the family meal to provide specific instruction that parents can then generalize to meals at home. A good example of this in a session is when the clinician "noticed" that the gravy family brought was sitting on the table untouched, using this as an opportunity to emphasize the caloric density of this food, praise the parents for bringing it and encourage them to incorporate it into their child's meal. The clinician then used this example to generalize to a discussion of similarly dense food items (oils, butters, nuts) as a point of parental education. Specific discussions about nutrition should include the frequency of meals/snacks, increased portion sizes for meals and discussions of caloric density. Helping parents reorient to what the patient liked or enjoyed before the ED assists them in externalizing around food choices. Additionally, these discussions are directed at parents, not the patient, so the supervisor will need to be aware when a clinician feels compelled to include the adolescent in this conversation, which may occur more commonly for novice FBT clinicians who are used to working with individuals. In many instances, clinicians are reluctant to step in to help families with their renourishment efforts. A primary goal of the session is to help caregivers figure out how to work as a team to increase their child's nourishment. Thus, the first order of business is to insure that the family has provided sufficient nourishment. If a family plates an insufficient amount of food, it is critical that the clinician act relatively quickly to help the family plate appropriate portions/foods. Waiting until the end of the meal to help provide additional food is not helpful to the family. In other words, once the food is plated, providing direct feedback on amounts and types of food is ideal. This, in and of itself, is often sufficient to help incite the ED and help the clinician and parents identify the ED-driven behaviors they will face as they challenge their child's illness.

Supervisory Intervention

In preparation for the session, new clinicians often need more explicit training on the nutritional needs of individuals with restrictive EDs. FBT clinicians are by no means expected to be experts in nutrition, but generally have an idea of how to support families in increasing nutrition to support weight gain. Thus, for all clinicians, we recommend you provide general guidelines around how to assess appropriateness of parental refeeding efforts with the foregoing stated goals in mind. In review of the meal, supervisors should ask clinicians to recount what parents brought, encouraging them to highlight parental strengths in responding to the directive to bring a nourishing meal, and places where knowledge is missing. This is also an opportunity for supervisors to correct misconceptions about appropriate nutrition. For example, some clinicians may feel uncomfortable with the quantities of food required to sufficiently refeed a child who is starving. Others may have their own preconceived notions about what is healthful (e.g., may comment on parent choice of soda for beverage). Supervisors remind clinicians that their own personal preferences and values around food and eating are not brought to bear on parental decision making, emphasizing again the importance of parental empowerment. Of course, if families are questioning a choice about whether to bring soda versus milk, the clinician might suggest that milk has a range of healthy nutrients and calcium, which may also promote bone strength (and thus have an opportunity to remind parents of the health consequences of starvation).

A Basic Primer on the Nutritional Needs of Individuals With Restrictive Eating Disorders

There are three primary ways families can increase nutrition over the course of a day. These include:

1. Increasing caloric density, which means adding high-fat, high-calorie foods. Examples of calorically dense foods include full-fat dairy products and the use of oils in cooking.
2. Increasing the frequency of meals presented. It is recommended that families serve three meals and 2–3 snacks daily.
3. Increasing portion sizes. Here the clinician can use other family members as points of comparison. It is notable when families serve identical portions and foods to each family member. This is an opportunity to teach about individual needs in the context of health, as well as an eating disorder.

There are many ways clinicians can educate themselves about how to provide adequate nutrition for their patients. Some patients may be coming to outpatient treatment from higher levels of care. In these instances, we recommend obtaining access to historical treatment records to assess recommended nutritional meals/sample meal plans. In an ideal scenario, the family will have completed an interdisciplinary assessment in a medical clinic specializing in the evidence-based treatment of EDs, and will have had an initial nutritional evaluation as well. It is important for clinicians to understand that in cases where the broader team is not working from an FBT model, the recommendations and focus of medical and nutritional interventions may be misaligned. Thus, discussing the family's prior experience in ED treatment with regards to how the child's meal planning was managed is key.

Case Example

A new clinician came to supervision to report on one of their first family meal sessions, looking quite befuddled. The supervisor asked the clinician to share about the meal from start to finish, first asking what the family brought. The clinician stated, "I was at a complete loss"— the family (in this case a single-parent mother and grandmother who lived in the home) had brought their daughter a single container of fat-free yogurt. The supervisor and clinician then discussed how the session unfolded—the clinician had asked the parent to share what their preference would have been, noting that the choice must have been made on the ED's behalf, not their child's, taking this as an opportunity for externalization. From there, the session proceeded with the clinician asking the mother to serve her daughter the yogurt, which her daughter quickly ate without complaint, all the while remaining withdrawn and indifferent to her mother's words of encouragement.

Supervisory Intervention

First the supervisor worked with the clinician to diagnose the dilemma, here being that the family did not follow the task at hand and missed the opportunity to build mastery in the refeeding process, as they simply brought a food they knew the ED would be comfortable with. The intervention missed by the clinician was to provide the family with information on the nutritional needs of the patient. Further, the mother's response to the therapeutic injunction in Session 1 was also indicative of a challenge in her ability to use externalization in a way that empowered her to take control over the renourishment process.

Here, the clinician's question was, *What should I have done? I thought about rescheduling the session, or holding a nonfamily meal session but just felt stuck.* The supervisor highlighted the important learning opportunities for both the clinician and family in this scenario. For example, she reminded the clinician that this gave her important information about the level of parental empowerment, familial accommodation to the eating disorder and perhaps lack of knowledge of nutritional needs, generalizing toward common patterns among families at these early stages (in this case, the mother hoped that getting her daughter to eat a preferred food would be better than her not eating anything at all). They processed the clinician's shock, which was reflective of underlying judgment about the mother, *not taking AN seriously enough, and perhaps has her own issues with eating.* Processing the clinician's emotional reaction created space to build empathy for the mother in the service of facilitating a non-blaming view of the mother, and the supervisor highlighted an opportunity for the clinician to respond agnostically. Here the supervisor used questioning to ask the trainee to practice externalization in the service of reducing blame and retaining an agnostic stance, providing corrective feedback, *You know so well how to feed your daughter as evidenced by the many years she was a healthy, thriving child before this illness took hold. Now, AN has you hostage, convincing you that if you serve it what your daughter needs it will put her on a hunger strike.* Finally, they reviewed strategies to promote learning about nutritional needs and facilitate empowerment in helping the family to feed their daughter one more bite than she intended. For example, the supervisor encouraged the clinician to ask the mother to pick something from the canteen, revisiting the initial assignment; alternatively they might have asked the mother to review what she would have liked to feed her child, or perhaps even scheduled another session.

For additional guidance on how to deliver Session 2 interventions with fidelity, please see the fidelity coding framework in Appendix VI. The following interventions are bookmarked:

- Providing feedback to the family about weight
- Taking a family history around structure of meals
- Assisting the family in understanding the nutritional needs of the patient
- Aligning parents in renourishment efforts
- Assisting the parents in helping their child eat "one bite more"
- Empowering parents in their efforts to feed their child
- Modifying criticism
- Externalizing the illness
- Involving and aligning siblings in a supportive role
- Keeping the focus on eating disorder behaviors
- Remaining agnostic

6 Remainder of Phase I

*Sarah Forsberg, Kathleen Kara Fitzpatrick,
James Lock and Daniel Le Grange*

Background on the Remainder of Phase I

The focus in Session 3 (and the remainder of Phase 1) is on helping families to consolidate new learning as they work with the clinician toward increasing their child's nutritional intake and weight. Because families move at different paces, these sessions may vary somewhat widely in their presentation across Phase I. More experienced clinicians will thus acknowledge typical patterns and be able to more quickly identify unusual presentations or challenges that may inform their interventions. Setting up a structure for the remainder of Phase I is important, and oftentimes novice clinicians delve into these sessions without previewing for the family what they might expect as they move forward. Thus, supervision should parallel an introduction to this phase with families, by helping clinicians think through the structure of the session in advance.

Preparation for the Session

Phase I sessions begin with a review of weight progress over the week, and proceed with the aim of keeping a focus on familial efforts toward disrupting the patterns that maintain the illness. In this way, the clinician is interested in directing the focus of the session based on his or her assessment, in collaboration with the family, of areas of learning and challenge with regards to renourishment. While Session 1 and 2 have very specific foci, the remaining Phase I sessions are more interactive, and thus at times it can be easy for clinicians and families to stray and for sessions to feel as though they are meandering. Where clinicians place their attention and focus, the questions they ask and the ways in which they guide the sessions may vary depending on family needs. All the while, the clinician continues to keep a razor-sharp focus on parental renourishment efforts, identifying common barriers families face that may inform subsequent interventions (e.g., parents are not aligned, not sufficiently empowered, are critical of their child and need help with externalization, or are having difficulty in keeping a focus on refeeding in and outside the session). Some families will have more difficulty following the structure of these sessions than others, in which case clinicians may employ more overt strategies to guide the conversation, including interrupting and refocusing the discussion, clarifying treatment goals and reflecting back the agreed-upon agenda.

Clinicians will be more involved in structuring early therapy sessions, and at the same time, the goal will be to teach this structure to families, with the aim of parents taking greater responsibility for the agenda as these sessions progress. Families who understand and value the structure will often come prepared to discuss the specific challenges they faced with renourishment in the week preceding the session, and will have also thought through where they have progressed in their ability to effectively interrupt the eating disorder (ED). In early Phase I sessions, the clinician is attuned to the family's response to these interventions as a point of assessment of family needs/challenges.

Common family challenges to explore early on include:

- The family who reports progress, appears to be on board with the model, but whose child is not gaining weight, and remains challenged in identifying barriers to progress
- The family who is acutely distressed and disempowered and seeks very specific directives from the clinician
- The family who does not have confidence in the treatment, feels their child needs another treatment protocol and is concerned that the focus is solely on food and eating
- The family who is relieved their child is in treatment; however, they become very concerned the treatment is ineffective when they start to refeed and witness an increase in distress and previously uncovered ED behaviors.

As a supervisor, it is your job to guide the clinician in beginning to identify these familial patterns, which becomes easier as the number of families treated with FBT increases.

It may be useful to think about Phase I in different stages. Sessions 3 and 4 encompass the "orientation" stage in which families are just getting formerly acculturated into FBT. You will be able to gauge their understanding to some degree by the rate of weight progress early on, and get a sense of how they are organizing themselves around treatment and how they are coping with these adjustments. By Session 6, clinicians should have a good sense of how the family is adapting to the treatment. In many cases, families who are successful in refeeding may feel discouraged by an increase in ED behaviors. It is not uncommon for previously hidden/secretive behaviors (e.g., throwing food to the dog, self-induced vomiting) as well as new behaviors to arise as parents become more attuned during and after mealtimes. At this juncture, the clinician should have clarity on the level of commitment of the family to stick through these challenges and continue in FBT. As Phase I progresses, clinicians should be seeing positive movement, even in cases where weight gain is slower than typical; families who are acquiring new skills and persisting in their efforts can continue to progress and the clinician's job is to help the family work at their own learning "edge." Supervisors should prepare clinicians to evaluate the rate of progress, and especially for new clinicians, this may be more difficult given the limited context. Thus, as a supervisor you provide this context, following the weight chart with the clinician in supervision sessions. A strong prognostic indicator and goal of this phase is a minimum of 1–2 pounds of weight gain per week (with approximately 4–5 pounds gained by Session 4), and this is communicated with the family. The clinician should emphasize the consistent data, pointing to early weight gain as the best prognostic indicator (Doyle, Le Grange, Loeb, Doyle, & Crosby, 2010; Le Grange, Accurso, Lock, Agras, & Bryson, 2014). When weight gain is slower, in supervision, the focus is on barriers to progress, and when faster, on evaluating the extent to which this is actual weight or is fabricated in some fashion (e.g., water loading, placing weights in clothing).

A general outline of Phase I sessions follows:

- *Meet with the adolescent for the first 10 minutes, take weight and identify agenda items for the session*
- *Begin the family portion with discussing and sharing weight on the weight graph*
- *Use weight progress as a gauge for discussion, evaluate familial response to focus on challenges versus points of progress*
- *Set the agenda with a focus on expanding upon successes and eliciting family problem solving around challenges*

The following interventions/principles create the focus for the remainder of Phase I:

- *Providing feedback to the family regarding weight*
- *Directing, redirecting and focusing therapeutic discussion on food and eating behaviors and their management until these concerns are resolved*
- *Discussing, supporting and assisting the parental dyad's efforts at refeeding*
- *Modifying parental and sibling criticism*
- *Externalizing the illness*
- *Remaining agnostic to the cause of AN*

A detailed description of fidelity benchmarks can be utilized to serve as a guide to Phase I sessions and can be found at the end of this chapter.

Common Dilemmas

Assisting Parents in Working in Concert

Description of the Dilemma

The focus of this intervention should be on assisting parents in improving their communication to maintain a consistent front. This might best be embodied by the phrase "on the same line, on the same letter, on the same dot," and this is how many clinicians describe this to parents. However, for some families it may mean continuing efforts to get them to agree on the need for treatment, or the focus of this treatment. Parents may also express concerns related to the family meal and the presentation of these concerns can serve to unify parents. In ideal situations, parents enter Session 3 focused on working together with the clinician. In some situations, however, the family may present as aligned against the clinician. In this case, taking time to understand parental concerns and finding areas for common ground are important. In other families, parents may present unaligned with one another, and regardless of whether this represents a new challenge in the context of the ED or a continuation of prior relational difficulties, significant efforts should be made at aligning parents with the goal of renourishment.

Supervisory Intervention

In preparing for sessions, the supervisor might help the clinician think about indicators of alignment. On one extreme exist parents who are divorced and refuse to communicate outside a mediator; on the other are those parents whose strong alignment has not wavered in the face of the illness. More typically, parents respond to the ED differently and may become polarized, which becomes a source of conflict undermining their effectiveness in renourishment. As a supervisor you can ask the clinician to identify verbal and behavioral clues about parental alignment—for example, are parents sitting together, do they turn to one another, their child or the clinician for support and feedback, do they use "we" statements in reference to their partner, what is the tone of the relationship when differences do arise, and do they attempt to resolve these or get stuck in patterns of withdrawal versus attack/blame? Here the goal will be to teach the clinician how to attune to issues of alignment and pull parents together, rather than engage in behaviors that might facilitate parental divides (e.g., allowing one parent to dominate conversation, shifting topics in the face of parental disagreement, acknowledging the need for parents to "be aligned" without assisting them in working out what this means for their relationship and the refeeding process).

Ultimately, parental agreement on the need for meal monitoring, increasing food intake (and how this is done), decreasing physical activity and complying (attendance, participation) with therapy is required. Clinicians help parents understand their own communication styles, patterns of interactional behavior, with the aim of helping them shift those that interfere with their ability to agree about how to intervene around the ED. Some parents may need assistance setting up a more concrete structure for communication (e.g., using a Google doc to list meals or reactions, scheduling time to speak each evening or morning to identify challenges). Other strategies, however, may focus more on reducing conflict between parents, which may be a result of long-standing marital challenges or disagreements about the illness itself. In these cases, the clinician should avoid marital conflict issues (or refer to an outside couples' clinician as necessary). Reminding the family that their other disagreements are minor compared with their agreed-upon desire to save their child's life may help shift their focus to this more pressing concern. In supervision, the goal is to assist the clinician with consistent monitoring of parental alignment and use of problem solving to address any challenges.

REVIEW OF THE SESSION

In reviewing early Phase I sessions with the clinician, the supervisor will want to consistently inquire about parental alignment by asking questions such as:

* *In what ways are parents aligned?*
* *Where do they differ in their view of refeeding and styles?*
* *Do they acknowledge these differences, work them out together or become entangled in conflict?*
* *How do parents work together outside of AN?*
* *What was their parenting style like prior to AN?*
* *Do they still work together on non-AN parenting issues?*

Over time, the clinician should be able to identify any challenges in parental alignment independent of the supervisor's inquiries and understand how differences here impact the refeeding process. You will also attune to potential clinician behaviors that might unintentionally facilitate parental differences. Common pitfalls here include speaking frequently to one parent on the phone and accepting calls or emails in which the parent wishes to discuss the other's behaviors. Further, in session, the clinician may become an ally to one parent, typically the parent who is less critical, more empowered and able to externalize the child's illness. This dilemma typically reveals itself in expressions of criticism directed toward this parent in supervision. It is often useful in these cases to help the clinician explore his or her emotional reaction toward the parent, whereby these reactions are normalized. The FBT intervention that is often most lacking in this scenario is reshaping criticism. Where clinicians are new to family therapy, or may experience discomfort in addressing criticism directly for fear of ostracizing the parent, or not knowing what to say, they may instead ignore these behaviors yet become frustrated with the parent and experience a desire to protect the adolescent. Thus, in supervision, unpacking critical comments, understanding the origin of these, and helping the clinician to reshape them through modeling are an important intervention. When a clinician does this effectively, it also models for parents a new way of responding to unhelpful statements and conflicts, which frees up space to focus on the task at hand. There may be many other reasons that parental alignment is lacking, and the goal here is to help the clinician understand the specific barriers. An FBT principle that may be taught in the context of work around parental alignment includes *empowering parents*, which often means reducing blame (e.g., if one parent is feeling guilty, or is critical of his or her partner). Reducing or reframing criticism is often an intervention that may be utilized to support parental alignment. Further, parents may have difficulty aligning when one parent is able to use externalization effectively and the other is not.

It is generally a good idea for supervisors to review some of the therapy sessions to get a sense of the family as much as the clinician's understanding and application of FBT. Watching clips of a session together in supervision is an opportunity for the supervisor to point out areas in which parents are not aligned, for example. You can begin to plan with the clinician how to intervene to increase alignment. Strategies to facilitate alignment include:

- Descriptively and nonjudgmentally highlighting areas where parents are not aligned, communicating directly about the importance of alignment versus asking parents to reflect on the challenges this conflict presents in their renourishment efforts
- Highlighting parental strategies and strengths, supporting parents in problem-solving how they can take the best of each other's strengths to become a unified front
- Assisting parents in identifying barriers to alignment (being on the same page, same line, same dot)
- Facilitating communication between parents—for example, when a parent expresses a plan to implement a new strategy, encouraging the other parent to share his or her perspective
- Helping the family to observe their process by reflecting in the moment on patterns/cycles of interaction

Case Example

In supervision, Dana, a 12-year-old girl with AN (anorexia nervosa), was discussed as the clinician noted that the father was frequently getting angry with his daughter for acts of physical aggression during meals. As a result, he often threatened that Dana would be admitted to an inpatient unit, stating the family could not manage her at home. The parents were not aligned here, as the father's comments often occurred when Dana's mother was in the midst of refeeding her daughter, often quite effectively despite behavioral outbursts. In these moments, Dana would become increasingly agitated and refuse her meal altogether, reinforcing the father's belief that she needed an inpatient stay, which subsequently deflated the mother's sense of empowerment.

In this case, the supervisor asked the clinician to "diagnose" the issue by asking the clinician to think about the particular barriers to parental alignment, which in this case were seen not as endemic to the preexisting parental relationship (parents did not have trouble communicating about or working together on other parenting issues) but as related to AN and an imbalance in parental empowerment. The clinician was able to identify that the father felt disempowered due to uncertainty about his role during meals. The supervisor asked the clinician to consider barriers faced in therapy as well as in the family structure that challenged the father's sense of efficacy. In this example, they used collaborative problem solving to identify strategies to highlight and reinforce effective behaviors on the father's part, and to revisit externalization to help the father separate his daughter from the illness, particularly in moments of her behavioral outbursts and tendency to push her father away. Further, the supervisor asked the clinician to consider how to join the parents in this discussion, and inquired about the ways in which Dana's mother found her husband helpful so as to facilitate connection between the parents. The supervisor asked the clinician to engage in self-reflection about her challenges in getting parents on the same page. With this opportunity, the clinician identified her tendency to allow the mother to interrupt the father in moments when he became frustrated and critical toward his daughter, thus supporting an unhealthy coalition between mother and daughter, leaving father feeling excluded. Other mediums of supervision employed here included a review of audiotape to observe parental communication (verbal and nonverbal), and a subsequent role play to practice redirection of criticism in a way that did not isolate the father but assisted him in practicing externalization.

Maintaining a Keen Focus on Weight Restoration: Managing Distractions

Description of the Dilemma

Starting with Session 3, a considerable portion of the session should be spent focusing on food and eating concerns with only minimal time spent on niceties, scheduling and transitional topics of discussion. Discussions of comorbid conditions or causal factors should generally be minimized and redirected. The only exception to this is if the family has made excellent weight progress very quickly and has fewer challenges; in these cases it can be acceptable to focus on topics such as expected developmental progress.

In most cases there are many areas the family could focus on, and the clinician is tasked with helping the family to zoom in on agreed-upon ED-related goals. This is not to say that the clinician should tell parents where to focus, but skillful implementation requires the clinician to problem-solve with the family the areas in which their intervention and energy will yield the most effective outcomes. Generally speaking, this means focusing on increasing nutrition/nourishment rather than focusing on reducing agitation or unusual but not obstructive eating habits (cutting food into small bites). Another way of saying this is that no one will gain weight if they continue restricting but reduce exercise—increasing intake is a foremost goal.

Helping clinicians identify specific areas for discussion may support their own focus in the session, and these include direct discussion of the frequency of meals/snacks, increased portion sizes for meals and caloric density, and following medical advice around exercise, including schooling, disrupting exercise and calorie-burning activities (e.g., remaining unnecessarily chilled to burn more calories). Strategies may include identifying for parents the areas in which they are concerned about "pushing more" and how the clinician might help with this reluctance; identifying previously enjoyed snacks/food items—usually those that are higher-calorie—and assisting them in adding back these feared foods; continued psychoeducation around the ways in which ED symptoms may change as a result of renourishment efforts—such as new concerns being stated, or upset and threats from the child directed at one or both parents, for example. These should be reframed for the family where possible and placed in the context of the disorder.

Clearly, there is much to focus on when it comes to refeeding; however, often families and clinicians alike find other topics compelling enough that they become distracted. These topics include a child's distress, concerns about comorbidities, body image concerns, management of friendships in the context of the ED and other problem behaviors (substance use, school issues, impulsivity).

Supervisory Intervention

The key principle here is helping the clinician to remain agnostic, which involves the redirection toward current eating behaviors and renourishment efforts as well as avoiding discussions regarding causality, which is often inferred in these other topic areas. Supervisors watch for clinicians who become timid in their redirection of families, which often reflects deference to family members (or a misguided desire to empower parent decision making), and their own interest or background in other therapeutic modalities or conceptualizations of the ED. Thus, you may remind clinicians of the importance of overtly acknowledging the need to shift focus to management of food and weight, and assist them in identifying their own personal barriers to doing so.

You will note that the issue of distraction by other causal mechanisms was addressed in Chapter 4, given the importance of *staying focused on the ED from the very beginning of treatment*. If this remains a concern in Phase I, it is important to identify what is being left out in the therapy, and the particular clinician and familial barriers to remain focused on. In many cases, distraction at this stage is related to an incomplete understanding of the focus of FBT, a passive response on the part of the clinician to discussions of cause (or perhaps the clinician has engaged with families on these topics previously, thus reinforcing the family for bringing other topics to the session). When this happens in Phase I, it can also be a reflection of new challenges that have arisen in the context of renourishment. For many families, when the eating disorder resorts to new, more aggressive behaviors, families become concerned that their efforts are not working, or are making the situation worse. More seasoned clinicians are familiar enough with this process to realize that with greater pressure on the illness, other behaviors may arise as the ED becomes more desperate to maintain a foothold in the face of parental efforts. These may include development of other ED behaviors—purging behaviors, redoubled efforts at restriction and increases in exercise, including nighttime exercise or restless/agitated behaviors (e.g., walking or standing while doing homework or during meals). Reframing this as success in efforts to put pressure on AN can help some parents, but may also require the clinician to introduce strategies or thinking around ways to disrupt these behaviors (e.g., injunctions to monitor after meals to reduce purging).

One way that this can sometimes be stated is: "Outwit, Outlast, Outplay"—stolen from the show *Survivor* and adapted to FBT. *Outwit* means that parents will always be one step behind the AN: they may find that the more pressure they put on eating dinner, the harder it is to get breakfast in regularly, or that the more they are nourishing their child, the more there are attempts to exercise. It is critical to reframe this as progress, rather than the creation of more problems through treatment, as these new behaviors are a response to parental pressure to overcome the disorder. *Outlast* means that families are busy and have many tasks, challenges and activities, and few families can easily take the time to monitor all meals without making some sacrifices. Placing critical importance on early progress and the importance of short-term changes in routine to assist with renourishment can help families realize that little is as important in early treatment as taking the time to get meals in. *Outplay* refers to behaviors that distract from nourishment efforts: swearing, pitting parents against one another, raising issues of "fairness" and calling attention to the behavior of parents or siblings in efforts to distract from the ED are all areas in which parents "are being played" by AN and benefit from clinician redirection to the symptoms that are presenting the greatest challenge.

For new clinicians, the emergence of these behaviors can be alarming if they are not familiar with the common trajectory of change. Thus, in preparation, you can help clinicians anticipate challenges the family is likely to face as early as the family meal session. Role-plays can be useful in helping clinicians develop greater confidence in their ability to redirect families while maintaining a collaborative relationship.

When the Eating Disorder Is Driving the Ship: Helping Parents Become Sufficiently Empowered

Description of the Dilemma

There are many early signs that clinicians can be trained to look for that indicate lack of parental empowerment. These include:

- Parents defer to the adolescent around decisions related to eating. This may be seen outright in session when parents back down when the ED disputes their suggestions. It can be more subtle in that parents may not report to the clinician when the child eats on his or her own, or they may not share that they have been purchasing "preferred" and "healthy" foods to keep their child (truly the ED) happy.
- Parents overtly state they are unable to take over all meals. Parents may use language like, "I can't do it, she won't eat, nothing I do works, I'm not sure what more I can do, I can't force her." They may engage in reason giving when the clinician attempts to engage them in problem solving (yes . . . but she hasn't done it before; but there's no way I could get to his school for lunch). This may be due to parental anxiety, parental anger and/or lack of skill.
- Parents frequently reference alternative forms of treatment, including making requests for additional sessions, additional therapeutic approaches or a higher level of care.
- Parents "demand" that the clinician provide concrete solutions. In many cases, families struggle with the notion that they can find solutions within themselves. While this is done in active collaboration with the clinician, some parents may become frustrated by the reality that there is no one right way to refeed their child. Further, they may lose confidence in the clinician when he provides a suggestion that was previously ineffective, thus feeling more hopeless and losing faith in the therapy, while continuing to place responsibility externally.

Thus, in preparation for the session, the supervisor can prime the clinician to attune to these signals of disempowerment. Supervisors are aware that novice clinicians can become polarized alongside the family in this context, either seeking to reassure parents of their skill, without providing concrete guidance, or becoming overly prescriptive in efforts to respond to parental anxiety or frustration. The consequences here are that parents continue to feel helpless or alternatively overly rely on others to solve the problem of the ED for them.

Supervisory Intervention

Many FBT interventions support parental empowerment and should be highlighted in supervision. If parents are not sufficiently empowered by early Phase I sessions, it may be due to a number of issues, most likely an interaction of parental variables (sense of authority around other parenting issues, parental anxiety, etc.) and the clinician's response. Thus, the first step is to help the clinician "diagnose" the probable cause of disempowerment. Common culprits include the following:

- *Lack of weight progress is discouraging.* In the case where weight progress is limited, the supervisor will want to help the clinician identify barriers to parental empowerment around renourishment. Here, the focus may be on identifying parental strengths and challenges and the range of ED behaviors that need management, and supporting parents in narrowing the range of focus to promote successful interruption of a single behavior. Here, the clinician assists the family in building mastery by breaking larger goals into smaller steps in hopes that when a smaller task is successfully accomplished, families can use this experience to generalize to other tasks. To start, the clinician may be asked to identify family strengths that can be expanded upon. The clinician should also reflect on his or her efforts to reinforce effective parental behaviors and whether parents are receiving this feedback versus becoming stuck on perceived failures. Strategies here that may be useful include using metaphors (e.g., "*We may not know the exact combination of treatments to cure a specific cancer; however, that does not stop us from beginning treatment using the tools we know to be effective*"), helping parents plan ahead for the emergence of new behaviors when others are under control, and using externalization to remind parents of the strength of the ED.
- *Messages from other providers are mixed.* Oftentimes families are involved with various systems, which may include individuals who are not trained in FBT and at best subtly insinuate the need for reliance on expert opinion, and at worst make recommendations that directly undermine parental empowerment. Here, the clinician will need coaching around how to support the family in bringing together a team who is able align their message to families.
- *The family has past experience with inpatient or intensive treatment programs whereby parents were not as directly involved and not responsible for renourishment.* Alternative treatment modalities have varying philosophies on the role of parents in treatment, and can interfere with parental acceptance of responsibility and confidence. In the worst-case scenario, families feel

ostracized and blamed. It is often helpful to openly discuss these different philosophies, allowing families the space to ask questions, and to deliver the rationale for treatment in a way that matches the family's needs. Clinicians need to remember that families often have little experience with psychotherapy, and when they do, their understanding of the structure and focus of treatment may be limited. This is another place where FBT clinicians join families, by helping them become experts in their own treatment.

- *The parents have anxiety and lack confidence more broadly about parenting.* For some parents, they have struggled to parent historically and fall to the poles of being overly permissive versus overly authoritarian. Other parents have experienced little reason to invoke parental authority and describe their child as typically developing and compliant in advance of treatment. Generally, it is possible to find some parallel to limit setting around food/eating in past experiences (e.g., a time when the child did not want to go on a family outing, or refused to go to bed on time). Here parents may need to develop new skills, and normalizing this aspect of treatment is key to minimizing feelings of failure or frustration. In supervision, the family's past parenting strategies and effectiveness are explored to target specific challenge areas.

- *The clinician is overly directive and thus parents are "shaped out" of taking ownership.* In supervision, you will want to look for indicators that clinicians are taking an overly directive stance with parents. This can include an imbalance in problem-solving strategies by providing specific suggestions for the family at the expense of helping the family generate solutions. Further, you may hear clinicians saying, "I keep telling them the same thing. I have said it in so many different ways, and it still isn't sinking in." Oftentimes, this indicates acceptance of responsibility when the aim is to shift the onus to parents, while continuing to provide appropriate scaffolding of learning. The supervisor helps the clinician examine the potential consequences of these interventions on parental empowerment (e.g., parents become discouraged about treatment as the "expert" has not provided them with ideas that have worked). Further, you may work out a family problem in session, role-playing the clinician while the clinician role-plays the family, and vice versa.

When an Extinction Burst Is Something New: Managing High-Risk Behaviors

Description of the Dilemma

Another common issue that arises is the changing nature of the ED. As identified earlier in discussions of the sorts of behaviors that distract families from the task of renourishment, sorting through the extent to which concerning behaviors are manifestations of the ED or represent a more imminent concern is important. For some children, the kinds of behaviors that arise occur at the extreme end of the continuum and include active suicidality and self-injury, significant aggression and behavioral outbursts (destruction of property, running away). Identifying how to intervene will depend upon the conceptualization of these behaviors (Are they functioning to interrupt parental efforts to address the ED? Are they representative of underlying emotion regulation difficulties that had been managed by starvation, or some combination?) and the level of acuity.

Supervisory Intervention

In supervision the emergence of new and concerning behaviors should be prioritized. First, for those with less experience in FBT, highlighting the range of typical trajectories of response to parental efforts is useful; thus didactics and case examples might be used here. Second, while most clinicians will be sensitive to any safety issues, it is important to request that these be addressed in supervision as quickly as possible. Supervisors need to be aware of any safety concerns in real time and may be required to support the clinician in intervening. It is helpful to clarify how the supervisor would like to be contacted at the outset of supervision (see Chapter 2) when these concerns arise, as some clinicians may worry about inconveniencing supervisors by contacting them outside of normal business or supervision hours. Of course, some clinicians may be more sensitive to these concerns, having less previous experience assessing and managing risk independently. However, even in instances where the concerns that arise are within the typical range of response to parental refeeding, supervisors will want to be cautious not to discourage clinicians from using them as a resource to evaluate risk. We encourage you to think in advance about how you respond in these situations, your preferences around level of support for clinicians and how this might vary depending on the level of experience of your clinicians.

There are questions you can use to guide clinicians to think through level of acuity and risk to determine necessary intervention. Walking through a functional analysis of the behaviors is helpful. Questions may include:

- What was happening in the environment immediately before the behavior manifested?
- How did parents respond (reinforce or punish) the behavior?
- Is this consistent with past behaviors that predate the illness? (Is there a history of suicide attempts, self-harm, behavioral issues?)
- How long do the behaviors last (in the case of suicidal ideation, behavior indicates expression of ideation) and how are they resolved?
- Do these behaviors occur outside of parental efforts to refeed or interrupt ED behavior?
- What have parents tried to support their child? How effective have these efforts been?

- Are there any immediate safety concerns?
- Is there any indication of imminent risk that requires developing a safety plan or need for a psychiatric hold?

Here, clinicians may need additional training in risk assessment and management and thus should be introduced to additional resources outside of supervision (e.g., in cases where suicidality is enduring, has escalated, or there is a plan and/or intent, we recommend you provide clinicians with an evidence-based suicide risk assessment tool and review in detail in the supervision session).

Oftentimes in these cases, both clinicians and parents "back off" of their efforts to manage the ED. It is important to balance management of safety concerns with continued efforts to fight the ED, which can also be life-threatening. Parents can take many steps to ensure that their child is safe by making environmental modifications (removing means to self-injury/suicide, increasing monitoring, including searching personal belongings or the child's room, removing bedroom doors, bolstering support by calling a crisis team or the police if needed for safety reasons). Further if these behaviors are truly designed to undermine parental efforts, clinicians will need to help the parents understand this while redirecting any criticism toward the child (helping parents externalize here) for making threats. Parents and clinicians alike can still convey the seriousness of these threats, and strategies like extending (offering to take the child to the emergency room immediately for assessment) may result in the child backing down from previous assertions. Of course, this does not mean clinicians discontinue their assessment of risk, but take this into consideration in exploring the level of acuity. Further, as soon as safety concerns are resolved, it is important for clinicians to help families refocus quickly on management of the ED. The learning curve may be steeper for those clinicians who have not had much crisis management experience and the goal will be to support them in becoming adept at assessing and monitoring these concerns while facilitating consistent focus on the ED. There will be some cases in which the clinician may need to intervene to protect the child's safety, which may derail treatment of the ED temporarily (e.g., enacting a psychiatric 72-hour hold). Further, there are some instances in which additional treatments (medication management, additional individual therapy to treat comorbidities) are warranted. However, these additions are often more appropriate in Phase II of treatment once an adolescent has reached a healthier weight and has capacity to engage in therapeutic modalities requiring use of analytic thought processes.

Managing Expectations for Weight Progress

Description of the Dilemma

The tone of the session should be set by sharing the weight at the outset to guide the direction of renourishment efforts. In Session 3 and beyond the clinician helps the family track their child's trajectory rather than becoming stuck on single data points. Over time, the weight chart becomes more useful in gauging parental efforts as more data is accumulated. In supervision, clinicians also share the weight chart as the supervisor will monitor any anomalies around weight progress.

Other challenges that come up for clinicians around weight include managing parent and child resistance to weigh-ins, which tend to manifest early in Phase I. If not well prepared to manage these concerns, parental and child discomfort can quickly convince clinicians not to share the weight, acquiescing to parent/child requests for modifications to weighing. Thus, in supervision, typical management strategies can be shared in advance with clinicians. In the vast majority of cases, sharing the weight with the child and the entire family is of utmost importance. As a supervisor you will want to address any hesitation and anxiety around collecting weight early in supervision.

Supervisory Intervention

Here, the goal is to help the clinician understand the central role of weight in treatment and its management. The supervisor cannot emphasize the importance of taking weight enough, and this can be done through an early focus on understanding the context of weight progress. In this way, supervision mirrors the work clinicians must do with families in the session as they guide them in using weight as a marker of progress. Thus, from the beginning of treatment, and early in Phase I, a discussion about weight history with clinicians is critical and includes:

- Reviewing growth charts
- Gathering history on the trajectory of weight loss
- Reviewing expectations that may have already been set by medical professionals
- Assessing family ideas about weight gain

This is especially important for novice clinicians, who may feel uncomfortable discussing weight with families, and may have difficulty making interpretations about weight progress especially when it does not follow an upward trajectory of 1–2 pounds per week.

Clinicians must be able to provide direction to parents, referring to the importance of knowing, understanding and analyzing weight changes to focus the session. It may not always be essential for patients to know their weight (more on that later) but it is critical that the clinician and the parents know the weight. Having a weight taken at consistent times and on a consistent scale is indispensable to this treatment. It is important that clinicians help parents understand that a medical weight answers different questions than therapy weights—these weigh-ins are not used to determine medical stability but are used to guide the current treatment session. Thus, communicating to your clinician the reasons weigh-ins are important is key. For example, spacing weigh-ins means we may miss behaviors or changes in weight that are important in evaluating overall efforts. Using a weight from another source also means we do not have opportunities to discuss things such as water loading or weight loss. In addition, parents often feel like there is a big focus on weight at the outset of treatment and they need to be reassured that this is one measure, albeit a very important one, of overall health and hence the focus. Finally, while patients are often weighed frequently at the start of sessions, when they are likely having more frequent medical follow-up, medical appointments are often spaced differently than therapy visits and what appears efficient at the outset can later become cumbersome or unrealistic (say, using a weight from the doctor a week before the session or not having a weight at each session). Knowing the potential pitfalls can help guide decision making early on.

Exposure and provocation are also important concepts in FBT. Although many parents feel their children become unduly upset when they know their weight, most patients already know their weight and most are quite obsessed with these numbers. Rather than avoiding these, however, the clinician can help the family reframe, noting that seeing their weight on a consistent basis in the face of eating disorder thinking can support treatment goals. Specifically, the goal is to help them see that the amounts that they are eating are translating into slow, steady weight gain. This is an opportunity for teaching the clinician about the kind of eating disorder–specific cognitions that can be addressed through this behavioral strategy (e.g., highlighting the differences between eating disorder expectations—"I gained 10 pounds this week! My parents fed me like a pig!"—and reality, which is often substantially less weight gain than expected by the patient). Patients often think that weight gain will be exponential when in reality it most often is highest at the outset of treatment and drops off. This helps reinforce the trajectory and expectations of treatment as well (Phase 1 focuses on weight gain and stabilization, Phase 2 is less about weight gain and more around flexibility and expansion of eating behaviors, Phase 3 is not about weight or weight gain at all).

Finally, the notion of provocation is an important one to review in supervision. In many treatment modalities the goal is often to better regulate the emotions and symptoms of the patient. However, in FBT the goal is to help parents engage with the ED directly and taking weight can often invite the ED into the room. This provides opportunities to coach parents in how to manage this pattern directly and with specific examples (see use of "bottom-up" opportunities to shape behaviors from Session 2). This can be disconcerting to families, and sometimes to novice clinicians, who prefer that therapy remain a calm and controlled environment. The drawbacks of this are that we cannot coach parents in managing more challenging behaviors, in tolerating distress, and in achieving a sense of ecological validity to our sessions. The goal is not, of course, to unnecessarily distress patients, but we must also assume that the healthy part of our patients is present (albeit usually silent) in these early sessions. Helping parents learn to manage the most challenging behaviors of the eating disorder without becoming critical of their child is essential. This is accomplished through therapist modeling a non-critical stance, and promoting the parents' skills in specific techniques to shape the disorder-maintaining behaviors. This can be framed for clinicians as an opportunity to help empower parents in using strategies such as externalization, redirection of criticism and others that directly address the manifestation of the illness in the session. You may wish to help the clinician identify language through the use of role-plays in supervision to enhance confidence in responding to these concerns.

COMMON CHALLENGES TO WEIGHING

Second, you will want to preview the challenges that arise around weighing and sharing feedback about weight with the clinician. For example, patients may manipulate their weight by water loading, loading their clothing with weighted items, or screaming/yelling/ or throwing tantrums around weigh-ins. These behaviors typically arise at Session 3 or later when patients learn the "rules" of treatment and can develop time for responding. For the first two issues, a key goal is to take a weight that represents as close to a "true" weight as possible. This means doing clinic weights with relatively minimal clothing (t-shirts and pants; no shoes, sweaters, sweatshirts, hats, checking that pockets are empty, etc.). If a weight seems unusual, such as a rapid increase in weight, the clinician may take a weight again after making certain there are no scale abnormalities. Following that, when the weight is shared, you remind clinicians to ask parents directly if weight changes are in line with their expectations. If they are, but the clinician suspects weight manipulation, you can wonder about that with the clinician and inquire about how he or she addressed this in therapy. Commonly, clinicians fear implying to families that a child might be lying; however, this presents an excellent opportunity for externalization to highlight the difference between typical behaviors and ED-driven behaviors. Providing examples of language clinicians might use with families here is especially useful—for example, "*Sometimes in an effort to show weight gain, some kids drink or eat just before session . . . did you see anything like that before this session?*" or "*The eating disorder may make your child so fearful of gaining weight that it will go to great lengths to hide true weight.*"

Other indicators of weight manipulation can be previewed, including patient use of the restroom during the session, in which case clinicians can take a second weight to see if weight changes after urination. Given the potential physical consequences of water loading, these sorts of behaviors need to be taken seriously by the clinician, and parents may need forewarning about these risks as well so they can intervene appropriately. In this way, supervision focuses on highlighting medical risks the clinician may have as yet been unaware of, with the aim of heightening parent activation. This can often be addressed by noting, "*It can be important to watch for water-loading behaviors, including eating salty foods and drinking water before session, because these behaviors are quite dangerous and can cause death through heart failure. The kinds of things we look for are drinking water before sessions in order to "fill up" and there is often information online that can guide these behaviors, without acknowledging how dangerous they are. Have you seen anything that would make you think this is going on in your family?"* If yes, the clinician should ask them more about it; if not they will encourage parents to observe or monitor for excessive water drinking, excessive use of the toilet, or insistence on using the toilet after weight is obtained, for example.

Another challenge you may preview for clinicians is when patients weight themselves to inflate the numbers on the scale. With non-gowned weigh-ins it can be quite challenging to catch. Removing all excess clothing (apart from the minimum that can be worn to be considered a clothed weight) is important. Additionally, make certain shoes (and sometimes socks as well) are removed, and hats, scarves, phones and so forth are all removed from pockets.

Finally, helping clinicians identify when weight progress is not on track is useful. This is certainly evident if patients are losing or maintaining weight; however, there can be many variations and fluctuations that occur. This is where understanding the context—parental report of progress versus objective data to support this report, the potential for eating disorder behaviors to interfere, making it difficult for parents to evaluate progress themselves—is useful. As a supervisor, it is your responsibility to help the clinician interpret weight progress. Further, recent evidence suggests that early weight gain in treatment is a predictor of outcome at the end of treatment. For those who gain approximately 5 pounds by Session 4, the likelihood of full remission is vastly improved (Doyle et al., 2010; Le Grange et al., 2014). Therefore, supervision should focus closely on this marker early in treatment.

When Phase I Does Not End: Problem-Solving Barriers to Progress

Description of the Dilemma

The typical duration of Phase I in FBT is 8–12 sessions. There are certainly outliers—in one study, families who received 10 sessions of FBT fared just as well as those receiving 20 (Lock, Agras, Bryson, & Kraemer, 2005). The largest dose of FBT provided in an RCT to date has been 24 over the course of one year, with more recent studies providing 16, and response rates were similar in each of these trials (Lock et al., 2010; Agras et al., 2014). There are exceptions to this, however, and nonintact families as well as adolescents presenting with more severe eating disorder obsessions and compulsions are likely to need a larger dose to achieve similar outcomes (Le Grange et al., 2012; Lock, Agras, Bryson, & Kraemer, 2005). Further, there is no data to guide what to do for those adolescents who do not fully recover at the end of treatment. In supervision, you will be monitoring progress of the adolescent closely with the clinician, and there should be no surprises and therefore no sudden decisions around changing course. When progress is slow or limited in Phase I, this is a topic of discussion all along and as a supervisor you will be observing, with the clinician, potential barriers. These may include a focus on barriers to parental empowerment and challenges to management of ED behaviors, including familial accommodation and reinforcement of such behaviors (e.g., never fully taking control over the refeeding process, giving in to eating disorder requests). They may also reflect other factors that may make uptake more difficult (chronicity and severity of obsessive-compulsive symptoms, single-parent households or separated/divorced families). Thus, problem solving will require consistent assessment and clarification of family-specific barriers.

Supervisory Intervention

At the outset of supervision of a new case, the supervisor may find it helpful to review the patient and family characteristics that are identified moderators of treatment outcome to frame expectations. Of course, this is done with acknowledgment of individual differences that may not be detectable in aggregated datasets. Indeed, because there are many possible reasons for lack of progress, it is generally helpful to follow a structured format to assess for areas to refine intervention, and of course ultimately to decide at what point treatment should be modified. Unfortunately, there are no data at present to guide these decisions, and thus they are generally based on clinical expertise requiring the supervisor to have seen a wide range of cases as points of reference. Helping clinicians assess and articulate the challenges is the first step. Over time, as clinicians gain experience, they will have a more accurate sense of the kinds of challenges and setbacks that are within the normal range versus those that are outliers. In supervision more advanced clinicians will come to the meeting already having a sense of the dilemma, which often will include a reflection of their own personal challenges in moving the family forward in applying solutions to their problems. Until experience is accumulated, you will need to walk clinicians through the steps required to both clarify the specific barrier and identify appropriate next steps.

Once the dilemmas are clearly articulated, the supervisor may help the clinician role-play feedback to the family about their observations, with the aim of mitigating family criticism/shame. Further, the clinician is encouraged to reflect on his or her own challenges in helping move the family along. The clinician invites the family to engage in collaborative brainstorming to consider potential remedies to identified barriers and may encourage a parent to lead this process or take notes. It is often useful to remind both clinicians and families that there may be no one "right" way to respond to these dilemmas, yet the family and clinician can utilize previous learning and return to principles of the model to guide next steps.

The fidelity coding framework for the remainder of Phase I can be found in Appendix VII and covers the following interventions:

- Providing weight feedback to the family
- Keeping the focus on food and eating behaviors
- Facilitating parental renourishment efforts
- Engaging siblings in a supportive role
- Modifying criticism
- Continuing use of externalization
- Remaining agnostic

References

Agras, W. S., Lock, J., Brandt, H., Bryson, S. W., Dodge, E., Halmi, K. A., . . . Woodside, B. (2014). Comparison of 2 family therapies for adolescent anorexia nervosa: A randomized parallel trial. *JAMA Psychiatry*, 71(11), 1279–1286.

Doyle, P. M., Le Grange, D., Loeb, K., Doyle, A. C., & Crosby, R. D. (2010). Early response to family-based treatment for adolescent anorexia nervosa. *International Journal of Eating Disorders*, 43(7), 659–662.

Le Grange, D., Accurso, E. C., Lock, J., Agras, S., & Bryson, S. W. (2014). Early weight gain predicts outcome in two treatments for adolescent anorexia nervosa. *International Journal of Eating Disorders*, 47(2), 124–129.

Le Grange, D., Lock, J., Agras, W. S., Moye, A., Bryson, S. W., Jo, B. & Kraemer, H. C. (2012). Moderators and mediators of remission in family-based treatment and adolescent focused therapy for anorexia nervosa. *Behavior Research and Therapy*, 50, 85–92.

Lock, J., Agras, W. S., Bryson, S., & Kraemer, H. C. (2005). A comparison of short- and long-term family therapy for adolescent anorexia nervosa. *Journal of the American Academy of Child & Adolescent Psychiatry*, 44(7), 632–639.

Lock, J., Le Grange, D., Agras, W. S., Moye, A., Bryson, S. W., & Jo, B. (2010). Randomized clinical trial comparing family-based treatment with adolescent-focused individual therapy for adolescents with anorexia nervosa. *Archives of General Psychiatry*, 67(10), 1025.

7 Transition to Phase II

Sarah Forsberg, James Lock and Daniel Le Grange

Background on Phase II

Phase II is about taking the management of food and eating that was handed over to parents in Phase I, and gradually shifting it back to the adolescent. This gradual shaping toward full independence can vary significantly from family to family, child to child. These sessions tend to focus on supporting the family in assessing markers of readiness for transition, developing successive steps that the child can begin to take in managing eating-related behaviors, and supporting learning and modification as needed. The aim is full return to independence that matches developmental expectations (e.g., a 12-year-old may only be eating lunch on their own at school, while an 18-year-old may be in charge of all meals and snacks with the exception of established family meals).

Early in training, it is very important for the supervisor to model active tracking of readiness for transition to Phase II with the clinician. Markers of readiness include sufficient weight progress (typically obtaining approximately 90%–95% of expected body weight), cognitive restoration (adolescent is more engaged in treatment, and able to make some healthy decisions) and emotional response (level of distress and associated eating disorder (ED) behaviors surrounding mealtimes have decreased). In addition, the supervisor is able to hold the typical trajectories of treatment in mind and translate this context into observation of points of divergence in a given case. As evaluated in randomized clinical trials, Phase II typically begins around Session 8, after 2–3 months of treatment.

Evaluating Readiness for Phase II

Supervision should then consistently take a bird's-eye view in assessing where a family is in the trajectory of treatment. Regular assessment of progress in supervision serves as a parallel process to the open review of progress in session, where the clinician reflects and shapes family process.

One strategy to insure consistent monitoring of progress is to review the following list of questions with the clinician in supervision, which serves as an evaluation of readiness for Phase II. These questions may be provided to clinicians early in treatment to facilitate their own monitoring and identification of areas of focus in supervision. Further, adolescents and their families may complete routine outcome monitoring measures that assess change in ED symptomology. For example, the ED-15 is a brief measure designed to capture change in core ED pathology session-by-session (Tatham et al., 2015). The Eating Disorder Examination-Questionnaire (EDE-Q) can be used on a monthly rather than weekly basis as it inquires about ED behaviors and cognitions over the past 4 weeks (Fairburn & Beglin, 1994). When using symptom-tracking measures, we recommend integrating feedback to families as a part of an initial review of progress. Clinicians should be one step ahead of the family to best prepare them to determine readiness to integrate increased independence, and these methods of assessment aid in this process.

Phase II Readiness Assessment

1. What is the rate of weight progress?

    a. Is the adolescent gaining 1–2 pounds per week?
    b. At the current rate of progress, how long would it take the adolescent to reach 90%–95% of expected body weight?

2. How is the adolescent engaging in treatment?

    a. Is the adolescent able to participate in healthy discussions about weight, eating and exercise?
    b. Is the adolescent expressing motivation to engage in typical activities that were arrested in the context of the ED?

3. How has the adolescent's response to mealtimes shifted?

    a. Is the adolescent experiencing any changes in his or her level of distress?
    b. How has his or her behavioral response to mealtimes changed?
    c. Is the adolescent continuing to negotiate and bargain around food choices?

4. How have parents responded to treatment?

    a. Do parents feel empowered/a sense of relief in successfully learning to manage their child's illness?

A NOTE ON MANAGING A CHANGING THERAPEUTIC RELATIONSHIP

Throughout FBT the therapeutic alliance is apt to shift and change, specifically with the adolescent. Early in treatment, adolescents may be entirely consumed by their illness as manifest in cognitive features, like inflexibility, lack of central coherence (overfocus on details) and difficulties with perspective taking. It is important for clinicians to understand the dilemma of engaging an adolescent whose sense of self and thinking is otherwise shrouded by his or her ED. Clinicians may be relieved to know that with renourishment, adolescents often recover their cognitive abilities, allowing for greater separation from their illness and engagement in the treatment process. The unveiling of a healthier, more flexible mindset is often a promising sign that an individual is making progress in his or her recovery. Many adolescents are able to comprehend the rationale for parental authority at early stages as they progress in treatment, thereby allowing space for the clinician to foster a stronger therapeutic alliance with the healthy adolescent in later stages. Clinicians can assist this process by assisting adolescents in externalizing their illness. Around the time of transition to Phase II, adolescents may be able to highlight ambivalence and separate thinking that is driven by their eating disorder from that which is in line with health. Clinicians need to pay attention to this gradual shift as it presents an opportunity to further align with and enhance the healthy side of the adolescent. While therapeutic alliance scores between clinician and patient early in treatment have been demonstrated to be lower than parent–clinician alliance in this model, there is room in treatment for building a stronger relationship as the adolescent continues to heal.

An early indicator that adolescents are approaching readiness for Phase II, as noted earlier, is the ability to on some level appreciate the need for recovery—adolescents may begin to express doubts that the ED can continue to serve them, and perhaps may articulate the ways in which it has gotten in the way. Further, they may begin advocating for greater independence in areas that are consistent with the developmental tasks at hand—for example, many adolescents express a desire to spend more time with friends, go on school outings and participate in sports or sleepovers. The time at the beginning of the session may be spent expanding upon adolescents' interests outside of their ED and encouraging exploration so long as it does not interfere with an ongoing focus on maintaining and regaining health as needed. In supervision, the supervisor might encourage clinicians to reflect upon changes they have noticed in adolescents, identify their strengths and interests, and potential gaps in developmental skills that may be addressed in later stages of treatment to buffer against relapse. Examples of skills deficits commonly seen among individuals with restricting EDs occur in the area of social skills—the ability to communicate needs effectively, fear of mistakes or failure, conflict avoidance, low self-esteem and lack of self-confidence, for example—that impact peer and other relationships. At the beginning of Phase II sessions, the clinician may take some time to highlight these skills deficits that may be addressed in greater depth toward the end of Phase II, early Phase III.

In some cases, developing a strong therapeutic alliance may pose a challenge. In our experience, this often is a reflection of the adolescent's difficulty in using externalization to understand the dilemma parents and clinicians face early on in removing control over eating, which may leave an adolescent angry and confused, viewing the clinician and parents as aligned around goals that are counter to his or her own. This may reflect a more ego-syntonic process, or perhaps parent–child conflict that predated the illness, or may be a reflection of an authoritarian parenting process. On the other hand, this challenge may reflect difficulties the clinician has in moving flexibly between highlighting his or her support of the healthy part of the adolescent and modeling firm limit setting with the ED. Alternatively, the presence of concrete thinking, severe ED cognitions that persist despite weight progress, and additional comorbid psychopathology could pose barriers to engaging the adolescent in treatment.

Common Dilemmas

The Transition to Phase II Happens Too Quickly

Description of the Dilemma

Identifying the root causes of the problem of the Phase II transition happening too quickly is the first step toward supporting therapeutic interventions to remedy this before a major setback occurs. More often than not, the following factors precipitate this premature shift:

- *Families are encouraged by their child's progress and become overly optimistic in assessing their child's capacity to be independent.* The more FBT cases clinicians work with, the more evidence they have about the variability in response to different challenges associated with treatment. The clinician here may help parents understand that the eating disorder has its own limits—and we may not fully know or be aware of these until we bump up against them.

Case Example

Janie, a 12-year-old, was very compliant with parental refeeding efforts—the clinician and family believed she experienced a sense of relief not to have to make choices related to food, and also preferred the internal conflict about eating arising within to the external conflict with her family. However, upon weight restoration and attempts to transition to Phase II, Janie was adamant about not wanting to make a "choice" for herself about meals and snacks. She preferred parental efforts as this provided an "out," allowing her to maintain her ED thinking through abdication of behavioral respon-sibility. In this case, the family was unaware of her internal struggle until the demands of treatment shifted. Upon transitioning to greater independence (parents started by allowing her to eat lunch unsu-pervised for the first time in many months), Janie quickly lost weight and her parents had to reevaluate her readiness. In this case, Janie met all of the benchmarks required for transition (was consistently compliant with meals, had reached 95% of her expected body weight), with the exception of her cognitive process around taking greater responsibility.

Supervisory Intervention

The supervisor worked with Janie's clinician to frame this experience as a learning opportunity for the family, incorporating information gleaned through the "behavioral experiment" of allowing increased independence into treatment planning. The supervisor and clinician reformulated the work of Phase II as requiring the patient to "make a choice" and encouraged parents to target choices based on the extent to which these activated ED cognitions. They paired developmentally appropriate activities (e.g., attending a friend's birthday party), with required steps toward independence (eating a piece of cake with friends). This hierarchy was constructed in supervision, and then tested through exploration with Janie and the family.

In Janie's case, her motivation to feed herself came from her desire to participate in social activities; thus these often provided a venue to prac-tice new independent eating exercises. School events involving food were opportune in that they allowed for parental monitoring, Janie preferred to "appear normal," and the family could predict to some degree the type of food available, thereby planning in advance with Janie. In this way, parents shifted to a model of shared responsibility that was less alarming to Janie in her ambivalence around making eating-related choices.

In addition, the supervisor encouraged the clinician to attend to the fam-ily's sense of pacing in introducing new challenges. Janie's family tended to overestimate her ability to succeed, given her general compliance and his-torical success in other areas of self-directed behaviors, and when Janie was unable to meet demands, would quickly become baffled and express a sense of helplessness around identifying a more appropriate next step. In supervi-sion, the clinician role-played providing feedback to the family on these observations, given the clinician's concern for the family's sensitivity to per-ceived criticism. The clinician was able to use directly observable behavior in the session to guide his reflections to the family about their process, encour-aging them to consider internal barriers to allowing for normative errors in the process. These parental patterns were first identified in supervision through a series of behaviorally focused assessment questions the supervisor posed. As a result, the clinician was able to share feedback with the family while supporting their sense of self-efficacy in regrouping and modifying their approach. The family was able to accept these challenges as crucial to their data gathering and development of new skills, rather than experience them as failures.

Managing Family Burnout

Description of the Dilemma

This is likely to occur in cases where Phase I extends longer than typical, and families are experiencing burdens in other domains of life (e.g., are unable to work, feel unable to care for other household and child-rearing responsibilities, feel unsupported by their partner). These contributors to parental burnout in treatment require careful monitoring and problem solving from the very beginning of treatment. It is normal for parental energy around refeeding efforts to ebb and flow. If parents begin to provide leeway to their child too early in treatment, this is typically revealed through poor weight progress or weight loss, or increased room for negotiation in session. Thus, in keeping the focus on eating and related behaviors early in treatment, the clinician will work with the family to identify gaps in their management of the ED.

Supervisory Intervention

In supervision, it is helpful to normalize parental challenges in refeeding so as to prevent parallel clinician burnout in attempts to activate parents and move treatment along. Empathy for families may often need to be actively cultivated throughout treatment, and supervision is an excellent space for this to occur. As a supervisor, maintaining an empathic stance toward clinicians who may be experiencing their own frustration toward parents (e.g., in instances where decisions about increased independence are made without consultation in treatment) is important. This stance opens the door for conversations about how to move beyond frustration to understand underlying parental motivations and challenges resulting in precipitous decision making.

Case Example

In the case of Tony, age 15, weight progress had been steady, albeit slow. His mother, who was a single parent of three, had been actively refeeding him for four months to get him to approximately 90% of his expected body weight (up from 75% following a hospitalization). She had initially taken a medical leave of absence from her job, and rearranged her schedule in returning to work to ensure she could go to school for Tony's lunch. Unbeknownst to the clinician, she had been experiencing increasing pressure at work to attend meetings in the afternoon, and felt she had less reason to excuse herself now that Tony was more medically stable. As a result, she decided to stop going to lunch with Tony, instead increasing his afternoon snack to account for the possibility that he may not complete lunch unsupervised. Tony's weight ultimately began to dip, which brought to light this recent change.

In supervision, the supervisor encouraged Tony's clinician to explore his perspective on Tony's readiness for some degree of independence given his steady weight progress and duration of treatment. She asked Tony's clinician to reflect on other markers of progress and resources available to the family to facilitate the mother's need for additional support. Further, there was space for exploring possible challenges to the therapeutic relationship that may have kept Tony's mother from sharing her plan with the clinician. The clinician recognized that he had not acknowledged the mother's concerns about her return to work, given the focus on charging her with the task of renourishment. By processing in supervision, the clinician was able to return to the session and address his having missed the mother's need to problem-solve in this area. In doing so, this invited the mother to share more openly about her level of stress in managing competing demands with limited support. The session was spent identifying alternative means of fostering independence that would allow for Tony's mother to meet work obligations. For example, it was determined that Tony could eat lunch with the supervision of his school counselor. Further, a close neighbor friend who lived nearby agreed to have Tony over after school to spend time with her son who was the same age, and provided him with his afternoon snack. Tony appreciated having increased time with peers and was able to successfully complete his snack in this new context. Further, while he was unhappy about eating with the school counselor, this provided incentive to work toward earning trust to eat on his own, which he achieved more quickly, given his increased motivation at this stage of treatment.

The Clinician Pushes Too Soon for Independence

Description of the Dilemma

As adolescents are renourished, improvements in thinking, reemergence of adolescent personality and interests outside of the eating disorder are encouraging signs of recovery. When an adolescent becomes more engaged, it is only natural for clinicians to wish to expand upon this engagement and facilitate appropriate autonomy with the aim of a return to normal developmental trajectories. Late in Phase I, if adolescents are progressing well, there should be observable improvements in affect regulation, their expression of interests outside of the ED, perspective taking and flexible thinking. In some cases, adolescents are very committed to returning to a sense of normalcy (e.g., wish to return to a favorite sport, having greater freedom in interacting with peer groups, and less involvement from parents). When this occurs, it is not unusual for clinicians to be convinced by these changes at the cost of understanding remaining ambivalence around giving up the ED. The shift in balance in negotiations between parent and teen can be confusing for clinicians and families. It is important for clinicians to maintain a cautiously optimistic stance with teens and parents. This involves noting their confidence in an adolescent's desire to gain a sense of normalcy and engage in behaviors that facilitate movement in this direction, while simultaneously acknowledging the barriers the ED may put in place, and planning in advance for these challenges. Ultimately, at this stage of treatment the decision about steps toward independence still rests with parents in consultation with the clinician.

Supervisory Intervention

In supervision, framing decisions about appropriate steps toward independence as learning opportunities is especially helpful. As supervisor, you will remind the clinician that all decisions can be reversed, that the purpose of trying new challenges is often to assess underlying readiness and barriers to change. Clinicians and parents alike may not have full information to predict the outcome of their choices. Thus, the supervisory stance is one in which missteps are expected and are utilized as important therapeutic material to shape learning and problem-solving capacity. If clinicians are comfortable acknowledging what they do not (or did not) know in supervision, this should translate to work with families. In the event that the clinician encourages relinquishing control in an area the adolescent is not yet ready for, the principle of externalization is useful. The adolescent's healthy motivation to return to independent behavior (e.g., spend a night out with friends) can be contrasted with the power of ED cognitions when eating what friends are eating (out at a burger joint), and without parental accountability in the moment. Separating the illness from the child at this stage of treatment can be challenging for parents who are relieved to see more of the child they know. It is common to see a rebound in criticism/frustration when their child is not able to manage newfound freedoms. The clinician can serve as a model to families in balancing a desire to promote healthy independence at this stage, while recognizing the need for a cautious approach given the relentless nature of EDs. Supervision can involve helping the clinician hold both the goal of interrupting remaining ED thoughts and cognitions, which requires parental involvement, and the goal of allowing for greater autonomy. Ahead are a few examples of this type of language the supervisor can model for the clinician in preparation for their work with the patient:

> *"It's so important for you to be out with friends, they matter so much to you, and it's so hard for you to challenge the ED on your own in these moments and eat what you need to be with them."*
>
> *"We all were rooting for you in having you try lunch on your own—it's so nice to catch up with your friends, and right now the pressure ED is putting on you is too high to not have someone else fighting it with you."*
>
> *"I recognize I got pretty excited last week thinking about you getting back to soccer, and because of my eagerness I didn't really consider how hard it would be to increase the food right now to be able to play. [To parents] What was your prediction about what this would be like for your daughter?"*

Determining Appropriate Scaffolding

Description of the Dilemma

The principle of behavioral shaping and building mastery is new to most families. In fact, many problems arise regardless of therapeutic approach when goals exceed capacity for success, leading to feelings of failure and limiting self-efficacy. Especially for families who are used to success, have high standards, or perhaps have less relevant experience in this area, it is important for clinicians to actively teach these concepts. At the same time, determining appropriate steps can be difficult, as the adolescent's skills to meet new demands have not been fully examined or tested until this juncture. As a rule of thumb, it is helpful to teach families how to apply the principle of building mastery, or building upon successive smaller steps toward a larger goal.

Supervisory Intervention

Clinicians early in training may also need some concrete examples to support parental decision making around the transition to greater independence. It can be helpful to think with the clinician about the end goals for the family (given family cultural background, developmental stage of the adolescent and prior family patterns). From there, you can work with the clinician to break each area of independence into a series of related steps. The following is an example of a primary goal broken into smaller tasks.

The goal for independence: Return to increased physical activity (e.g., playing soccer)

- Step 1: Allow for supervised and brief drills (within the realm of what is medically safe at home) (e.g., passing the ball back and forth for 15 minutes) without negative impact on weight. Parents will participate and/or monitor initially.

- Step 2: Allow to attend games and observe.
- Step 3: Allow to participate in warm-up (stretching, light jogging) for first 15 minutes of practice once per week to start.
- Step 4: Allow for increasing length of practice time.
- Step 5: Allow for increasing length of game-time play.

All the while, the clinician and parents are actively assessing the adolescent's success in managing these smaller steps. For example, if an adolescent cannot complete soccer drills without engaging in efforts to exercise compulsively (e.g., jogging in place the entire time despite reminders to remain stationary), it is likely parents will need to choose an easier step (e.g., allowing for supervised physical activity that was not previously associated with excessive exercise—e.g., going on a family walk). In addition, parents may learn that they need to be quite descriptive about their expectations up front, so their child understands what success looks like. This may seem like an incredibly incremental process, and for some adolescents this is required. Others may be able to take bigger steps if they demonstrate early success and their desire to participate in a specific goal is much stronger than their illness.

In supervision, a fun activity to support learning in this area is to take a specified goal and encourage clinicians to brainstorm as many iterative steps as they can think of. This is helpful when it comes time to model this kind of solution-generating strategy when parents become stuck in an all-or-none mode of thinking. It is a cognitive exercise toward skill building and also may highlight areas in which adolescents become stuck (i.e., they become perseverative in their desire to return to full participation or nothing at all).

The Transition to Phase II Happens Too Slowly

Description of Challenge and Supervisory Intervention

Typically when the transition happens too slowly it can be explained by the following:

- *The clinician is overly cautious and/or overly directive with the family.* Generally this pattern is seen more commonly among novice FBT clinicians who are reassured by parental oversight. In these cases, clinicians may also respond to parental enthusiasm and confidence in transitioning to independence with increased caution as a counterbalance. This polarization within the therapeutic relationship is problematic and must be addressed in supervision. Typically this is seen when parents begin to take steps toward independence and the clinician response is to view these decisions as irresponsible and hasty. Instead of eliciting parental rationale, the clinician response may be to overestimate the strength of the ED and need for parental oversight. Here, the principle of a consultative stance is quite important and can be emphasized in supervision.

This involves exploring alternative, more appropriate steps toward independence, reflecting and expanding areas of progress, and sharing creative ideas generated by other families in similar situations. It may be important to explore clinician anxiety, should this be a barrier to allowing space for trial and error (within reason).

- *The medical team is overly cautious and is making recommendations that coincide with the need for medical caution, but do not promote behavioral and cognitive growth.* In FBT, it is the clinician's role to educate the entire team about the psychological needs of the patient, provide a rationale for transition to increased independence, and set expectations around moves in this direction. With this context in mind, the medical team may provide consultation to the clinician on the types of steps that may pose a greater risk to medical stability. As families transition and determine how best to do so, it is important for the entire team to support these shifts. They can often be surprising and even alarming to medical teams when they have tapered the frequency of visits and thus may not have as accurate data on progress. Here again is a place where supervision should support the development of clinician confidence in taking a leadership role in liaising between other team members and the family. In parallel, clinicians may also work to coach parents to communicate their plan to the medical team, with the aim of incorporating data on medical risks/benefits of their decisions. Oftentimes clinicians may feel challenged in stepping into this role. Encouraging frequent contact with medical providers with the aim of facilitating positive working relationships is an important component of supervision. In supervision, working with the clinician to identify a plan for collaboration, assisting them in providing concise, relevant data to the medical team, and focusing on promoting parental decision making and efficacy are key.

- *The adolescent patient has not made weight progress in Phase I, or has made significant weight progress, but continues to experience distress around eating and fight parental refeeding efforts.* If the adolescent has been engaged in treatment for over one month with little or no weight progress, there is a need to reevaluate and identify alternative strategies (e.g., introducing adaptations to the model, adding an adjunct therapy or changing models). It would be unusual in these circumstances to work toward transitioning to Phase II. Adaptations to FBT for those families who struggle to make early progress in treatment are currently under study and involve reinvigorating family concern about the seriousness of illness, exploring barriers to parental alignment in a separate parent session and holding a second family meal. Further elaboration of these additional sessions is forthcoming, and preliminary data can be accessed in a feasibility study finding that those with AN who needed and accessed adaptations were able to get back on track with progress (Lock et al., 2015).

Case Example

Olivia was an 18-year-old with a 4-year duration of illness with two prior hospitalizations. Olivia was compliant in therapy sessions and willing to engage in discussions with parents about refeeding, recognizing her inability to restore weight on her own. However, while there was weight progress, and she was able to stay out of the hospital (Olivia gained approximately 2 pounds in the first month of treatment, and an additional 7 pounds in the subsequent 2 months), she was still severely underweight (approximately 80% of her expected body weight). The family was successful in monitoring her post-meals and Olivia had 3 months free from self-induced vomiting. While Olivia's weight progress was quite slow and she continued to struggle to eat all of the meals her parents provided, the supervisor and clinician felt hopeful about her progress in the context of her prolonged course and age. She was engaged in therapy and problem solving, and expressed a desire for greater independence, noting she felt "babyed" by her parents and "incompetent" in the sense that she was not able to go to school, be with peers and get her driver's license. Thus, the transition to Phase II in this case began with negotiating increased independence in areas of forestalled development (e.g., taking driver's ed, going to a café on her own). Eventually, this extended to inviting her boyfriend over for meals at home and eating out with him as she viewed him as a source of support. Weight progress remained halting and slow; however, Olivia expressed renewed hope for recovery and a desire to apply to college and move away from home. Thus, Phase II of therapy became a process of negotiating independence around eating through exploration of risks/benefits to her health and developmental trajectory.

In cases where there is a strong rationale to modify treatment, the aim is to uphold key tenets of the approach (e.g., in this case, parents were empowered and involved in a supportive role that facilitated maintenance of progress and medical stability, the family externalized her ED well, allowing them to separate healthy goals related to independence from ED thoughts and behaviors).

On occasion, adolescents are weight-restored by the time resumption of independence is considered, and even then they may struggle to take back responsibility over meals and snacks. When this occurs, understanding the extent of ED cognitions, the function of resistance to independent eating activities, and progress/challenges in other areas of development is useful.

Case Example

Sylvie, a 13-year-old girl with a history of atypical anorexia nervosa, had a promising early course of treatment. She had regained weight over the first month of treatment and returned to her previous growth curve along the 75th BMI percentile. Further, she had resumed menses and the focus in Phase I had shifted to prioritizing normalized eating patterns rather than continued weight gain. She ate what her parents served with little resistance. While the clinician and parents felt ready to encourage the practice of independent eating behaviors, Sylvie became withdrawn and refused to communicate her goals related to independence. The clinician and family became discouraged by Sylvie's reluctance, deciding to continue for a time in Phase I to determine whether with additional practice she may become more cognitively ready to shift to Phase II. They continued in Phase I for another two months of treatment, at which point in supervision, the supervisor raised concern that there were no observable signs of readiness for Phase II (Sylvie remained shut down whenever family attempted to discuss opportunities for independence). Further, Sylvie continued to become emotionally dysregulated (crying uncontrollably) every time the clinician took her weight, despite very minimal fluctuations around her estimated healthy weight. Thus, while physically and behaviorally she demonstrated readiness for Phase II, she continued to exhibit behaviors suggesting a struggle with the cognitive effects of her ED.

In supervision, the supervisor asked the clinician to conceptualize the barriers to moving forward. This included a review of the clinician's understanding of underlying ED cognitions and the function of the ED in the family system. During this process, the clinician realized he, and the family, had a relatively limited understanding of Sylvie's inner experience, as she had historically been reluctant to share about her ED, lending to her tendency to comply rather than elicit conflict. In the interest of shifting to Phase II and to elicit greater participation from Sylvie, the clinician chose to increase the amount of individual time from 10 to 20 minutes over the next two sessions. These meetings helped confirm two hypotheses the clinician made—namely, that Sylvie felt that her ED was the only aspect of her personality that made her "special" in the context of a history of social anxiety and social withdrawal. Further, she experienced significant fear that she might overeat and gain weight to the point at which she would be ridiculed and reminded by her doctors that her weight was in the overweight/ obese range (she had previously tracked along the 95th percentile, had a history of teasing and medical interventions targeting weight loss). The clinician learned that Sylvie enjoyed the comfort of having parents manage her meals as it both alleviated anxiety about further weight gain and protected her from having to venture out of her comfort zone with her peers (she would no longer have an excuse for not eating lunch with peers, which was highly anxiety-provoking).

With this additional information, the clinician and supervisor developed a plan to gradually increase independent eating behaviors, with more intensive scaffolding from parents initially (e.g., parents insisted that Sylvie plate her own food, and subsequently provided feedback/ made adjustments, they gave her 2–3 options for snacks that were already in Sylvie's repertoire, and arranged to have meals out with family friends who had children Sylvie's age, to give Sylvie practice eating in front of others). Sylvie preferred to "fit in" and thus did not want parents to choose her meals during these occasions; this provided an excellent incentive for Sylvie to practice developmentally appropriate independence. During the individual time prior to family sessions, the clinician began to provide education to Sylvie about social anxiety, and assisted her in developing basic anxiety-management skills in line with goals Sylvie set (e.g., wanting to develop peer relationships). Eventually, as Sylvie became more engaged at school and attended a two-day school trip, she became increasingly motivated to eat on her own. She was reassured by the stability in her weight despite making some initial choices on her own, and became more willing to take risks with regards to her eating.

This case illustrates the importance of ongoing assessment in FBT when progress is stalled. Here, spending more time with the adolescent to obtain clarity in case conceptualization allowed the clinician to design precise interventions targeting the underlying barriers to full recovery. As noted, increasing individual time in Phase II can be a helpful way to engage more of the healthy part of the adolescent in problem solving and identifying his or her unique goals for independence. Eventually, the clinician referred Sylvie to a cognitive-behavioral therapy for social anxiety group, as Phase II was nearing completion and the family was identifying goals for Phase III, a primary goal being to assist Sylvie in building confidence in her relationships and decreasing avoidance that perpetuated her social anxiety.

References

Fairburn, C. G., & Beglin, S. J. (1994). Assessment of eating disorders: Interview or self-report questionnaire? *The International Journal of Eating Disorders, 16*(4), 363–370.

Lock, J., Le Grange, D., Agras, W. S., Fitzpatrick, K. K., Jo, B., Accurso, E., . . . Stainer, M. (2015). Can adaptive treatment improve outcomes in family-based therapy for adolescents with anorexia nervosa? Feasibility and treatment effects of a multi-site treatment study. *Behaviour Research and Therapy, 73*, 90–95.

Tatham, M., Turner, H., Mountford, A., Tritt, A., Dyas, R., & Waller, G. (2015). Development, psychometric properties and preliminary clinical validation of a brief, session-by-session measure of eating disorder cognitions and behaviors: The ED-15. *International Journal of Eating Disorders, 48*(7), 1005–1015.

8   Phase II Issues

Sarah Forsberg, James Lock and Daniel Le Grange

Background on Phase II

The focus of Phase II is still very much on management of ongoing eating disorder (ED) behaviors, and ensuring maintenance of weight progress toward a healthy weight range. However, families present with wide variability in their mastery and understanding of ED behaviors, the ability to balance independence goals with management of eating pathology, and the ability to apply skills acquired earlier to novel challenges. As noted in the previous chapter, Phase II is an excellent opportunity to learn more about aspects of the ED that remain untouched or unaffected by parental refeeding efforts to date. In helping the adolescent eat more and more on her own, it is expected that new roadblocks presented by the ED will need to be addressed. Thus, to some degree, Phase II requires greater flexibility on the part of the clinician and parents to modify their focus and strategies to facilitate a return to normal adolescence and full recovery. The primary foci of Phase II are as follows:

- Continued parental management of ongoing ED symptoms until the patient demonstrates ability to eat independently and gain/maintain a healthy weight.
- Return to developmentally appropriate independence in a gradual fashion.
- Exploration of the intersection between developmental challenges/ skills deficits and ED pathology to solidify Phase III goals.
- Continued family skills-building to facilitate return to a healthy developmental trajectory.

A general outline of Phase II sessions is as follows:

- Meet with the adolescent for the first 5–10 minutes to obtain weight and identify agenda items for the session (★Note: occasionally the initial meeting with adolescents extends due to their increasing engagement with treatment. This is a helpful time to explore readiness to transition and identify adolescent-specific goals regarding desired independence.).
- Provide feedback to the family regarding weight.
- Direct, redirect and focus therapeutic discussion on food and eating behaviors and their management until these concerns are resolved.

- Discuss, support and assist the parental dyad's efforts at refeeding where required.
- Continue to modify parental and sibling criticism, especially as it relates to understanding challenges in returning control over eating to the adolescent.
- Externalize the illness—revisit the discussion of ongoing aspects of the illness, current healthy behaviors and their overlap.
- Keep agnostic focus, while identifying the ongoing function of remaining ED symptoms as they relate to key adolescent developmental challenges.
- Problem-solve with the family to create a behavioral plan toward increased independence and evaluate and reformulate this plan as needed.

Eating disorders disrupt relationships and participation in academic and extracurricular activities, and prevent acquisition and mastery of new skills required to develop a healthy relationship with oneself and others. Adolescents are expected to struggle with the return to a more typical developmental trajectory, and as demands increase, setbacks can be anticipated. It is most important in these scenarios that parents and families learn to *adjust*, *acquire* and *apply* new skills and subsequently *assess* their efficacy:

- Parents *adjust* by incorporating new information about their child into their conceptualization of the current state of illness.
- Parents *acquire* new skills by exploring what has worked previously and how these strategies map onto the current situation, and modifying or learning new approaches.
- Parents *apply* the agreed-upon approach.
- Parents *assess* the efficacy of their intervention to determine whether further modifications are required, and incorporate their learning into future planning.

Supervision in Phase II often mirrors families' learning as new demands in treatment emerge that may challenge clinicians. Often, the sense of urgency that supports an extreme intervention (full parental control) is no longer present, and facility in negotiating this grey area is aided by exposure to a wider variety of cases and a strong background in adolescent development. Thus, in early supervision with more novice clinicians, supervisors often return to a more didactic style as they seek to assess and fill gaps in knowledge. It can be helpful to engage clinicians in an exercise designed to evaluate the patient's current recovery status, barriers to progress (ongoing and predicted in the context of shifting independence structures), family strengths and remaining challenges that require focus in order to support recovery.

The following structure and case example may be useful in reevaluating treatment goals at this stage and utilizes the principle of externalization to separate ED behaviors from those aligned with healthy development.

Phase II Treatment Goals (Appendix VIII)

	Example	Where/when are these present	Where/when are these absent	Treatment goals
Ongoing eating disorder behaviors.	Secretive exercise (crunches, jumping jacks in room).	This is an ongoing compulsive behavior that increased in response to removal of participation in sports at initiation of treatment.	When playing soccer, the patient did not engage in these behaviors; however, soccer eventually became an opportunity to engage in compulsive exercise.	Return to healthy physical activity 1. Assess motivations for return to sport. 2. Identify steps toward gradual return to sport while monitoring pathological exercise. 3. Encourage parents to revisit strategies for increased monitoring of secretive exercise.
Body image concerns	Patient engages in frequent body comparisons with friends (in person and on social media) and verbalizes distress about weight as compared to friends.	These behaviors intensify in the context of a peer group that engages in discussion about dieting and body shape/size.	Events precipitate body comparisons frequently throughout day. Screen-time is limited when patient is doing homework.	Decrease frequency/impact of comparisons.
Developmental strengths	Patient is able to verbalize consequences of comparisons and frustration regarding societal standards of beauty and recognizes this behavior as problematic to her recovery. Patient is social and has a diverse and supportive group of friends.			
Developmental challenges	Patient relies on validation from peers, has low self-worth and has excessive self-standards, leading to frequent perception of failure			
Parental strengths	Parents have balanced expectations for achievement and encourage patient to practice flexibility and spontaneity. Parents model effective communication.			
Parental challenges	Parents have difficulty setting limits around typical adolescent behaviors and identifying consequences to problematic behaviors (e.g., frequent angry outbursts with parents and siblings during periods of heightened anxiety/stress).			

This evaluation can occur through direct observation of behavioral and cognitive patterns in-session and through objective measurement utilizing standardized ED measures (e.g., the EDE-Q or ED-15, referenced in Chapter 7). The supervisor assists the clinician in organizing and prioritizing goals to design focused interventions. This formulation is revisited and modified at each meeting and allows for identification gaps in the clinician's understanding of ongoing ED concerns and their relationship with developmental tasks. It also helps keep the clinician and family focused when treatment goals may have otherwise been ill-defined.

Common Dilemmas

Knowing When to Align With Adolescent Goals: Continuing to Separate Disordered From Healthy Behavior

Description of the Dilemma

This dilemma was introduced in Chapter 7, as shifts in the therapeutic relationship/alliance are common at this stage of treatment. The initial individual time with the adolescent in Phase II is a rich opportunity to build rapport, understand motivations and challenges and collaboratively set goals.

Before discussing where clinicians get stuck, understanding how this space can be used to propel family work is important. In the majority of cases, the clinician is able to use this time to elicit and normalize ambivalence related to full recovery, to support the adolescent in building motivation. Further, adolescents may begin to use this time to "test" their own thinking by sharing concerns with the clinician in this safe space, prior to doing so in the family meeting. It is the clinician's job to reassure adolescents that the aim of treatment is to facilitate their management of eating, so long as it is consistent with health-related rather than ED-related goals. Here, adolescents are encouraged to identify their own recovery-oriented goals, which can support problem solving around the steps required to reach such goals. Further, when barriers to these are met, it is an opportunity for the clinician to support adolescents in exploring the impact of the ED on their broader interests and goals.

Adolescents may have difficulty effectively communicating their needs for independence, and typically continue to experience distorted thinking (difficulty with perspective taking, future orientation and analytical thinking). As such, the clinician can begin to identify these challenges with the patient modeling alternative viewpoints as a means of facilitating effective communication. While the goal will be for parents to help their child with this skill, this may be an area of difficulty for parents too. Parents may need assistance differentiating normative assertion of divergent viewpoints from those that facilitate the ED. For example, an adolescent may take an "all-or-none" stance (e.g., "If my parents won't let me eat dinner at my friend's, there's no point in going at all"), which can be viewed as an attempt to assert developmentally appropriate autonomy versus the eating disorder's attempt to regain control over a particular situation (or some combination therein). Clinicians and parents alike are apt to struggle to make this distinction, especially early on. Negotiation within limits is actually encouraged in Phase II, and here the clinician helps the family integrate divergent perspectives to guide decision making. This is a point of divergence from Phase I, where negotiation is overtly discouraged in the context of more fully consumed ED brain.

As described in Chapter 7, the difficulty many clinicians run into is how to balance the development and maintenance of a trusting relationship all the while remaining vigilant to ED signs and symptoms. Most clinicians enjoy their work because they are reinforced by patient improvement and recovery. Seeing more of the adolescent (i.e., getting to know his or her unique strengths, interests, personality outside of the illness) is incredibly rewarding for most clinicians and families alike, as the adolescent is no longer so medically fragile at this point in time. This can lead to a tendency to overlook the areas in which the adolescent continues to remain ill, or to minimize concerns in light of progress. This not only has significant consequences in terms of attaining a full recovery but also can impair both the adolescent and family's trust in their clinician, if they are missing important information.

Supervisory Intervention

In supervision, the supervisor is actively monitoring patterns in clinician behavior. If, for example, it appears that the clinician "takes sides" or expresses polarized beliefs about the transition to independence, it can be helpful to note these and ask the clinician to reflect on his or her own experience. The supervisory interventions that are most useful here are encouraging self-reflection, modeling self-reflection (the supervisor can express his or her own reaction to clinicians' report of their impressions and interventions) and continually revisiting the conceptualization of the adolescent's current status.

Case Example

In one case, it became apparent in supervision that the clinician consistently nudged parents toward allowing their child greater independence. When the mother identified concerns, the clinician would encourage the mother to explore her own personal barriers to giving more freedom. In supervision, the supervisor asked the clinician to share her underlying experience of the family that contributed to her tendency to reframe and reorient parental concerns (encouraging self-reflection). Through this conversation, the clinician was able to identify feeling pushed by the mother herself, and noted concern about the mother's response to anxiety, which was to panic and resume full control. The clinician felt that this pattern was unhelpful and preventing the adolescent from taking ownership of her progress and kept her from sharing openly. The clinician also reflected that the interventions she was using to address this dynamic had the unintended consequence of decreasing the mother's confidence in the clinician. Once the clinician identified her own pattern of behavior, she was able to modify her approach. In session, the clinician used self-disclosure to highlight her tendency to become polarized in her thinking with the family and her assessment of why this pattern ensued. The clinician stated, "I have been spending a lot of time thinking about how I can do a better job supporting your daughter's transition to greater independence, while decreasing risk for return to ED behavior. I noticed a pattern I think may be happening in our relationship and am wondering if I can share this with you?" By sharing the work she had done outside of the session, the clinician was able to join with the family and invite them into the process of problem solving. The family thus approached this conversation with openness and a sense of curiosity about their own behaviors. From here, the clinician provided feedback on specific interactions in the session in which she experienced a desire to push for greater independence. From here, the family and clinician explored new ways of responding to this pattern and a plan for monitoring in future sessions. The family agreed to work on the skill of tolerating uncertainty in taking risks, while the clinician worked to meet the family in their desire to take the transition toward independence more slowly.

Reintegrating Sports, Exercise and Other Physical Activity

Description of the Dilemma

Many young people are engaged in physical activity prior to the development of their ED. For others, exercise and participation in sports emerge around the onset of illness, and become a symptom promoting the ED. Understanding the progression from healthy to unhealthy exercise and its temporal relationship to the development and maintenance of the ED provides the groundwork for a plan to build physical activity back in. Leading a physically active lifestyle has many benefits, including promotion of self-confidence and self-esteem, overall physical health, stress management and facilitation of social connections. Therefore, an active lifestyle runs the gamut from riding a bike a brief distance to school to competing in elite athletics, and discussions about the patient's goals should be carefully integrated throughout the latter phases of treatment. It can be confusing determining how to best hand back physical activity and it is very often integrated either too quickly or too slowly. Further, this is a place where team members can become polarized. Medical team members may apply physical standards of health to set goals for return of physical activity (e.g., require specific medical thresholds are met, and make recommendations about the duration and frequency of physical activity). While this is a critical aspect of the assessment, it represents one piece of the puzzle in determining how to proceed. The missing piece in this equation is an understanding of the potential cognitive and emotional factors that may contribute to a patient's readiness to engage in activity. Clinicians are charged with encouraging families to integrate indicators of medical readiness with an understanding of their child's mental and emotional experience around physical activity. They should be in close communication with other team members to insure all aspects of readiness are integrated to support parental decision making.

Supervisory Intervention

In supervision, you may ask the clinician to take a thorough assessment of historical exercise patterns as they relate to the development and maintenance of the ED. The following questions may be posed to clinicians in supervision to aid in this evaluation. Further, these questions may be utilized in session with families to encourage families to process the complexities of this choice.

- What was the nature of the adolescent's physical activity/exercise prior to the onset of the illness?
  - Was the adolescent engaged in healthy physical activity?
  - Did the exercise patterns arise in the context of the ED?
- What aspects of his or her exercise patterns are disordered?
  - Did the adolescent exercise in a compulsive or rigid manner?
  - Did the adolescent stick to a strict exercise routine/pattern?
  - Did the amount (frequency and intensity) of the exercise increase?
  - What was the function of exercise?
  - Was exercise used primarily as a means of shape/weight control?
  - Was exercise used as "punishment" or compensation for eating?
  - How did the adolescent respond to limitations on his or her exercise? For example, did the adolescent experience significant distress or guilt?

- What aspects of the adolescent's exercise were healthy?

  - Did the adolescent differentiate between healthy/unhealthy forms of exercise (e.g., was his or her participation in a sport done in a healthy manner while engagement in calisthenics at home was disordered)?
  - In discussions with the adolescent, to what extent is the adolescent able to distinguish between healthy/unhealthy exercise patterns?

- What are the risks associated with introducing exercise?

  - Vulnerability to compulsive behaviors, desire to do more
  - Weight loss associated with difficulty adjusting to new energy needs

- What are the potential benefits associated with introducing exercise?

  - Increased socialization
  - Increased self-confidence
  - Improved body image; reprioritization of function of body
  - Increased motivation toward recovery with achieving goal of participation in sports, for example

These questions support both the clinician and family in generating solutions surrounding reintroduction of exercise. They also highlight the complexity surrounding this decision, thus encouraging preemptive strategies to facilitate a successful transition. Once the family determines their priorities surrounding reintroduction of exercise, the clinician's job is to encourage successive steps toward mastery. As discussed in Chapter 7, engaging in physical activity is not an all-or-none phenomenon.

Case Example

To illustrate, Anthony was a 12-year-old boy who initially developed his eating disorder in the context of excitement surrounding his newfound talent for running. Anthony received significant praise for his skill from peers and family members, where otherwise he experienced anxiety and low confidence in his social and academic life. His exercise behaviors quickly became compulsive to the extent he was pushing himself to go above and beyond track requirements by adding an additional hour of training, which eventually turned into two and then three hours per day. In treatment, Anthony was most disturbed by the removal of physical activity and asked his parents daily to return to exercise. While he wished to return as quickly as possible to cross-country, he also expressed a desire to play soccer, which he had historically played with his brother and neighborhood friends for fun. The family was understandably nervous about allowing Anthony any physical activity, for taking it away had caused significant conflict in the home, and for a long time, Anthony was exercising in secret despite parental limit setting. However, Anthony had restored nearly all of his weight toward the beginning of Phase II, and given his age and the family's cultural preferences around mealtimes, there were limited domains in which to increase independent eating. The family struggled to identify steps they felt would facilitate return to healthy exercise, and were often immobilized by their anxiety about re-inviting conflict into the family. With encouragement and exploration in therapy, the family decided to allow for supervised family physical activity, which served multiple functions. By exercising together, the family could safely monitor Anthony's behavior and end the activity if he appeared to be engaging in a compulsive manner. Further, the family found this was a pleasant means of building connection and routine and creating a healthy lifestyle together. This context modeled for Anthony an alternative function of physical activity (emotional well-being and family connection) that expanded his own cognitive frame-work. As Anthony was able to engage in a healthy manner, the family slowly began to increase the duration of their activity, and moved from low-impact exercise (walking in the park) to higher-impact activi-ties (riding bikes and kicking a soccer ball). From there, Anthony was allowed to join the soccer team, although the family first discussed limitations on his participation with Anthony and his soccer coach. At first, Anthony had a modified practice schedule (decreased fre-quency and duration), and slowly built up to full participation in both practice and games. His father was the assistant coach and thus was able to monitor his participation. Anthony was aware that continuing in soccer was contingent on maintaining a healthy weight range, eat-ing what his parents provided and decreasing compulsive behaviors. The family occasionally chose to limit Anthony's participation as a natural consequence to setbacks. For example, they decided to allow Anthony to choose his snacks after he began soccer, and when they made this change, Anthony lost some weight. The family modified their approach to giving Anthony specific options to choose from that better met his nutritional needs in the context of increased physical activity.

This case vignette illustrates a single path toward return to exercise, and there is significant variability in how families approach this task. Changes in physical activity are also complicated by an often simultaneous increase in independence around meals. It can be helpful for families to work on 1–2 changes at a time, so they are positioned to modify in light of setbacks. For example, when exercise is introduced, parents may require their child to have an additional snack and maintain supervision for a time to ensure energy needs are balanced. Adolescents commonly have difficulty increasing nutritional intake to offset energy loss, and thus the risk is that they may lose newfound privileges around physical activity. Ideally, the clinician should help the family preemptively plan for energy deficits and identify strategies to increase nutrition to encourage forward momentum. However, this is often a part of the learning process as families and clinicians alike gather information about how an individual's body responds to these changes.

In supervision it is important to preview the risk for parents to rely on the clinician to make these recommendations. The clinician's job is to continually promote parent-empowerment and the consultative stance. The aim in defining this process is to assist the family in grappling with the different variables that make their child and their path unique. Clinicians may feel pulled to make recommendations; however, again, they should be reminded of the collaborative essence of FBT and help parents develop their own problem-solving capacities.

Stalling Out: When the Push for Final Weight Progress Plateaus

Description of the Dilemma

When an adolescent's weight plateaus or drops in Phase II, this typically signals the persistence of ED cognitions and that the chosen step was too demanding given the current state of recovery. It can be very discouraging for families to experience setbacks during this transition period, and especially difficult to remove newly gained independence.

Supervisory Intervention

Clinicians can assist families in anticipating the struggles their child may face in taking ownership over their eating and activity levels again. Similarly, the supervisor assists the clinician in predicting challenges and, when they arise, identifying likely contributors to weight loss or increases in ED behaviors. In most cases, if families are systematic in the changes they make with regards to independence, problem areas reveal themselves more easily. As families take bigger steps in the area of independent eating, they may be less certain about the specific issues. For example, the family who allows their child to simultaneously begin incorporating physical activity *and* eat lunch independently may be uncertain about aspects of the illness that are driving weight loss.

Thus, the focus of supervision at this stage is engaging the clinician in problem solving around the identified cause of setbacks. Further, it is important to note that the solution to this challenge may not be return to full parental control. Supervisors encourage clinicians to identify the smallest steps families can take to scale back independence, while maintaining progress is a part of the art form of this stage of treatment.

Young people who are more engaged in therapy and transparent in their struggles may contribute their perspective about barriers to progress. However, it should be acknowledged that most still struggle given they are tasked with making healthy, non-disordered choices about meals for the first time in many weeks and sometimes months. In addition, patients are often nearly or fully weight-restored at this juncture, which can elicit newfound anxiety around "going too high" or "overshooting" a target weight range. Some have resigned themselves to obtaining a specific weight, but no more, or are reminded of being teased, uncomfortable or less confident at a specific weight. Clinicians can engage the adolescent and family in discussing weight goals openly and normalizing this concern.

If it becomes clear that an adolescent is unable to feed himself or herself adequately to continue to maintain or gain weight as needed at this stage, it is important for parents to continue supervising meals, while the adolescent may practice choosing among parent-approved options, or portioning with parental correction so they may practice independence in a safe fashion. Especially early in Phase II, it can be helpful for families to encourage independence when they are able to observe the adolescent directly. This is important given families may more directly observe challenges the adolescent faces (e.g., putting excessive emotional energy into deliberating between choices, consistently putting a much smaller portion than required on the plate). When this happens, parents can scaffold support and step in where the ED is activated (e.g., setting a time-limit on decision making, reflecting the adequacy of both choices, reminding an adolescent to add more to his or her plate).

Making Nutritional Adjustments to Support Weight Maintenance

Description of the Dilemma

In Phase II, the goal is to help adolescents attain a healthy weight range. In some instances, families are afraid to adjust the amount of food their child is eating given concerns for weight loss. For some individuals, this can have the unintended consequence of ongoing weight gain. Generally, utilizing historical growth charts and data, behavioral and cognitive observations, and other markers of medical stability to guide determining a healthy weight lends sufficient confidence to this determination. However, discussing concerns about "overshooting" a target weight can be a difficult subject for families and clinicians who may fear triggering the patient.

Supervisory Intervention

Here, the supervisor supports the clinician in beginning to have conversations with adolescents about their perceptions of their weight, their experience of ongoing weight gain and strategies to tolerate discomfort around feeding themselves given fears about excessive weight gain, for example. Talking with the family about their views about a healthy weight range allows the clinician to educate the family where there may be misconceptions, support the family in utilizing more objective data in identifying a healthy weight range, and support modifications to their feeding, for example. Adolescents may be invited to share their preferences for modification to the meal plan, so long as these suggestions are considered healthy. For example, an adolescent may state that eating a cheese omelet cooked in butter with a side of peanut butter toast and an orange juice leaves them feeling overly full prior to school. The family may consider alterations to this meal to respond to reactivated hunger and fullness cues. They might choose to cook two scrambled eggs without cheese, or the adolescent may choose a breakfast he or she would like to integrate into the rotation that provides sufficient energy (e.g., granola with Greek yogurt and fruit). Historical data can be very helpful in making these decisions assuming adolescents had a more typical or healthy relationship with food prior to their illness. Here, the clinician may engage family members in a discussion around what they imagine healthy eating will look like for their child in recovery. Patients may be asked to recall how they felt about their eating (e.g., likes and dislikes) prior to the ED. Reviewing the range of eating habits of peers and family members as diverse models is a ripe opportunity for observation of different viewpoints and the presence of unhealthy perspectives, and can instruct on what the range of "normal" eating looks like for those in a similar stage of development. It is important to highlight that nutritional needs for individuals with EDs may remain higher for some time, and specifically that energy deficits (e.g., unintentionally missing a meal/snack, getting sick and being unable to eat adequately, entering a new eating environment) can introduce significant vulnerability to relapse.

In supervision, clinicians may be asked to reflect on their own perceptions of normative eating behaviors, the family's preexisting relationship with food and how this has evolved over time in the context of treatment to prepare for a similar conversation in session. In Phase II, families often need guidance in articulating the range of normative teenage eating behaviors. Some families may have a steeper learning curve in readjusting to normative patterns of eating given conflicting sociocultural values around nutrition, their own biases and their anxiety in the context of their child's history. Clinicians remind families that they may not have all of the answers as to how healthy eating is defined for their child. At the same time, they encourage families to engage in behavioral experiments as they modify nutrition, knowing they will be collecting objective feedback in the session (i.e., through review of weight changes, their child's behavioral and emotional response). As sessions are spaced out in Phase II, parents are encouraged to monitor indicators of progress outside of weight, as this will be required throughout the remainder of treatment. For example, signs of a lapse or weight loss may include mood changes (increased irritability), food refusal, increased conflict around meals, return of ritualized eating behaviors, and avoidance of family meals. The goal here and throughout Phase II is to bolster families' confidence through creation of a framework they may utilize to monitor progress in the eventual absence of therapy.

9   Phase III and Termination

Sarah Forsberg, James Lock and Daniel Le Grange

Background on Phase III

Phase III typically begins when weight is normalized and the adolescent is able to manage independent eating and exercise patterns with limited interference by eating disorder (ED) cognitions. While we may hope for an adolescent to be free of all ED cognitions and behaviors, data suggests that cognitive recovery may lag behind physical and behavioral recovery (Lock, Couturier, & Agras, 2006). We highlight this finding to remind clinicians that treatment may be considered successful and complete even in cases where full cognitive recovery is still underway. In some cases, where significant distress or impairment is associated with cognitive symptoms, a slightly longer course of FBT (e.g., 9–12 months as compared to a standard 6-month course) may be useful, or the adolescent may be referred for an alternative treatment.

Whereby the focus of Phase II is return to autonomous decisions about food and eating, Phase III expands the focus toward management of adolescent developmental tasks. Further, just as a successful return to adolescent development is emphasized, so too is a return to a focus on the parental unit as one in which parents may continue to work together as a team around other issues. Phase III serves as an opportunity to remind parents that the skills they have learned to work together to resolve the ED may also be applied to other areas of conflict in their relationship and in their parenting. For single parents or nonintact families, the same process of broadening the skill set and maintaining an authoritative parental structure applies. Consistent with the goal of encouraging family autonomy, the therapy sessions in Phase III are spaced out to encourage families to gain confidence in their ability to manage concerns as they arise with less scaffolding by the clinician.

As originally written, Phase III is meant to be brief and focused on helping the family identify areas of skills deficits that may have contributed to the predicament of the ED initially, and may interfere with healthy development. As noted, a clear prerequisite for doing FBT is a background in adolescent development. Thus, when a family is first entering Phase III, the supervision should focus on a review of typical developmental milestones and features that fit the age (chronological and developmental) of the individual in treatment. Clinicians should have a conceptualization of behavioral patterns that predate the onset of illness and the extent to which these are developmentally normative (e.g., breaking household rules, risk taking, increased irritability) versus problematic in the ways they have manifested both through the ED and in the adolescent's life more broadly.

The tone of Phase III is also an important topic in supervision. You may recall that in the very first session parental anxiety is maximized toward action. It is the clinician's job to strike a balance between encouraging parents to face the seriousness of the illness and invigorating parents' capacity to take action. In Phase III, it is important for the clinician to keep a close ear to how parents are feeling about their child's progress and whether their emotional response is appropriate given remaining concerns. The tone of Phase III is much more optimistic and hopeful; however, the clinician is careful to balance this with an air of caution toward the risk of relapse in this population. Thus, the clinician will help families strike a healthy balance between the poles of blind optimism and exaggerated hypervigilance.

A Developmental Model: Understanding Developmental Stages and Tasks

A consideration of the clinician's development shapes early discussions about transition to Phase III that involves identification of family-specific goals. For those clinicians early in their training, with less formal experience in conducting treatment with adolescents or in a family context, it can be helpful to assign reading that provides a primer or summary of what is considered typical of adolescent developmental stages. We recommend the following article to our clinicians as it nicely delineates the tasks of early, middle, and late adolescence (Fitzpatrick, 2011). With more experience, clinicians might prepare a summary of the developmental tasks that would be expected and typical for a specific case that can be utilized in supervision to formulate Phase III goals. It is especially important to help the clinician explore and integrate cultural norms for developmental expectations as the family cultural background may not map directly onto expectations outlined in the culture where therapy is taking place (e.g., in Western cultures, where there is a value placed on individualism and autonomy). When clinicians have a solid foundation in adolescent development, they will be able to support families in observing and resolving conflicting goals.

Case Example

A clinician who was relatively new to FBT, although with significant background in treating adolescents, was assigned to work with a 15-year-old first-generation Taiwanese boy with AN raised in an intact family with one younger sibling. In supervision, the clinician first reviewed common expectations for an individual at this developmental stage, when peers continue to be more influential, and adolescents engage the development of abstract-thinking skills (e.g., may test parental and other adult authority). In Eric's case, the clinician observed that he had not followed this typical trajectory, and posited that he grappled with the dilemma of holding different views from his family. In fact, when he shared feelings of disappointment or sadness, or expressed his preference, he also experienced secondary guilt due to the perception that he was rejecting his family. His parents' differing views of his attempts at emotional expression reinforced this pattern. The father, who was fluent in English, actively encouraged and rewarded emotional expression and viewed this as a positive sign in his son's recovery. His mother, whose English was quite limited, responded in a way that indicated she felt rejected and at times disrespected by her son. These feelings were heightened when Eric expressed disagreement with her views. Further, this often incited conflict between parents as it highlighted their different views on parenting and development stemming from their own childhoods. The clinician was able to highlight the challenge Eric faced in developing a sense of security in himself given the inconsistent punishment and reinforcement he faced in expressing different viewpoints, preferences and emotional states. Determining how to best provide this feedback was a challenge as the clinician was aware of the ways in which the mother felt disempowered and criticized in her overall approach to parenting. Further, the mother's expectations were aligned with her upbringing, whereby questioning authority was a sign of disrespect.

In supervision, it was decided that rather than approach the family in a didactic fashion whereby cultural norms around development would be highlighted, the clinician explored the family perspectives on developmental expectations in their culture and family of origin. In doing so, the father was able to express empathy for his wife, given economic and gender differences that shaped their own cultural experiences, noting that she was expected to care for her family until she found a partner. Eric's mother expressed frustration at being asked to carry significant responsibility for caretaking in the family that left her feeling burdened. Given this unspoken expectation, she felt undervalued in the context of her son expressing his needs, which were then supported by her husband. Identifying these challenges in a nonjudgmental manner helped normalize conversations around an evolving and more aligned approach to parenting. Eric thereby felt more comfortable sharing his experience of feeling confused when presented with conflicting expectations. He shared with his parents that his teachers, while viewing him as an accomplished student, frequently marked him down on his ability to contribute to in-class discussions and debates. They frequently provided feedback that they wished to hear his opinion to better assess his reasoning, problem-solving and abstract-thinking capacity. Eric noted he felt shy and concerned that he might be viewed as disrespectful or that in expressing an opinion, he would unintentionally trigger conflict. The family was able to differentiate between conflict that promoted learning and growth and conflict that was experienced as unresolved in the family.

The next supervision session focused on helping identify strategies to teach the family effective conflict resolution and negotiation. The clinician asked the family to write a letter outlining where they would like to see their son at the end of treatment and a year post-recovery. This was an opportunity to identify parental discrepancies further and to encourage the development of Eric's own sense of self and goals for his own recovery.

In this case, the supervisor helped to structure the way information about developmental expectations was delivered with the aim of engaging parental discourse that highlighted differences within their family cultures and between their cultural upbringing and that of their son. Rather than instruct the family on expectations of the dominant culture, the tenets of parental empowerment and parental alignment were enacted in framing the discussion in this way. The supervisor was able to expand upon the clinician's strengths (his ability to conceptualize the developmental challenges in the context of the family's cultural background), and then apply these using principles of FBT.

Preparation for the Transition

Phase III Readiness Assessment

In supervision, one strategy to insure consistent monitoring and assessment of change is to review the following list of questions with the clinician, which serves as an evaluation of readiness for Phase III. These questions may be provided to clinicians at the outset of treatment with the aim of helping them self-monitor and identify areas of focus for supervision.

Phase III Readiness Assessment (Appendix IX)

Is the adolescent fully weight-restored?

1. If the adolescent is not fully weight-restored, what are the barriers? Is the adolescent actively engaged in working on the barriers and is he or she appropriately motivated in achieving full weight restoration?
2. Has the adolescent had sufficient practice with meeting the demands of independent eating?
3. Do the adolescent and family feel that goals related to independent eating have been accomplished? For example, does the family feel that there is a sense of normalcy around eating routines that reflect histori-cal patterns or desired patterns they have identified in the process of treatment?
4. Is the adolescent back to most if not all typical activities (attending school regularly, spending time with peers, participating in activities of interest)? If not, is this because of ongoing concerns for the ED, or due to other areas of challenge that may be addressed in Phase III?

If the answer to any of these questions is no, it is important to identify barri-ers to progress in the context of supervision. There may be occasions where moving to Phase III is indicated, even if the adolescent or family has not met all of the foregoing criteria. Specifically, when barriers to increasing independence are related to other skills deficits, the clinician may choose to move forward. For example, a young person who has difficulty with cog-nitive and behavioral flexibility (e.g., shifting a response to meet novel or unexpected demands) may be encouraged to practice this skill in response not only to food-related challenges but also changes in other routines. The family is thereby assisted in understanding areas of overlap between inde-pendent eating and skills deficits more broadly. Sessions therefore may focus on identifying related strategies to increase flexibility, spontaneity and deci-sion making in multiple domains outside of independent eating.

Common Dilemmas

Making the Transition Conscious

Description of the Dilemma

Throughout Phase II, assuming the adolescent continues to make appropri-ate progress with meeting new challenges in independent eating behaviors, it is not uncommon for other topics to be introduced by the family or clinician, as noted earlier. This can occur quite naturally, as all parties may feel more relaxed, and other areas of concern may feel more pressing once the initial crisis of the ED is resolved. Thus, especially for those clinicians who are newer to the approach, the shift in focus toward other topic areas can happen without consciousness. It is important to create a structure for this transition for a variety of reasons:

- Families feel empowered to consider how they would like to focus their remaining time in treatment.
- Families will be able to further hone their skill of prioritizing concerns and aligning their focus.
- The clinician can guide the family toward areas of concern that may have been vulnerabilities to the ED that affect the adolescent more broadly.
- The emphasis can be placed on addressing areas of skills deficits in development to protect the adolescent from relapse.
- Families and clinicians can negotiate goals and use their time efficiently.
- Families and the clinician are clear on the remaining structure (timeline, frequency and goals of treatment) and have an opportunity to discuss termination.

Supervisory Intervention

As highlighted earlier, clinicians should be tracking potential areas of focus for Phase III throughout treatment. Therefore, supervisors provide an orientation early in supervision to common concerns and developmental challenges arising in this population, while remaining keen in their focus on helping parents disrupt ED behaviors in the first phase of treatment. Clinicians should be encouraged to bring these observations to supervision so the supervisor can help them prioritize and keep their focus, while beginning to form hypotheses about future Phase III goals. Another challenge clinicians and families face is that they try to tackle wide-ranging challenges (e.g., comorbidities, more general family conflicts, preexisting challenges associated with temperament). Supervisors thus monitor for the tendency for clinicians to become distracted and/or overly ambitious in their treatment approach, which may be a reflection of family process and its impact on the clinician. This can be a more common challenge for novice clinicians, or for those who have backgrounds in various other training models and populations, and feel comfortable treating other issues. Supervisors remind clinicians that Phase III is not meant to represent a shift to a new treatment modality, or to tackle comorbid conditions, like anxiety and depression. When clinicians begin to drift in such a way, supervisors rein them back toward a keen focus on the goals of Phase III that will support ongoing ED recovery. When there are other areas of concern, like unresolved conditions, such as anxiety, depression or substance use, referrals to other providers may be warranted and provided at this time. Supervision once again parallels the family session in that the supervisor helps clinicians problem-solve around their priorities for Phase III and choose an area of focus that they believe is most relevant to helping the child most specifically with his or her recovery from the ED.

There may be occasions where the family clinician decides to continue working with the adolescent and/or family to address other problem areas. If the benefits of remaining with the FBT clinician are clear and outweigh potential challenges (e.g., in navigating shifting roles), clinicians will need to make a clear distinction in their role, differences in therapeutic frame and treatment goals. The supervisor will need to help the clinician think through such potential ethical dilemmas related to dual-role relationships, the therapeutic framework and importance of working within one's area of competency. Determining when to make a shift from FBT to a different therapeutic modality is also complicated by the potential for ED challenges to arise in the future. Thus, in supervision a clear plan around how the clinician will manage these roles is necessitated to facilitate clear communication with the family before any changes are made.

The foregoing readiness assessment can be provided to clinicians in the form of homework for supervision and may be useful in guiding their own thinking on an individual's readiness. Ahead we highlight typical areas of focus in this population for review in supervision, with suggestions on how it may be utilized to identify Phase III goals.

Understanding Adolescent Issues

Description of the Dilemma

In order to work well with adolescents and their families, clinicians must be grounded in child and adolescent development. Having a developmental framework in mind at the beginning of treatment will help clinicians and families in distinguishing between typical behaviors and those that are cause for concern, as are ED behaviors. We encourage trainees to read some basic primers on adolescent development, as one of the initial tasks of Phase III is to give an overview for parents, so the clinician and family can think together about where their child sits in this trajectory, and the ways in which the ED has led them off track. It is important to assist clinicians in increasing their comfort level with discussing topics like sexual maturation and relationships, experimentation with drugs and alcohol and other risk-taking behaviors that may be more characteristic in teens. As clinicians delivering this treatment it is important to be able to recognize potential bias that may stem from one's own personal values, cultural background and upbringing, for example. It is typical for teens and parents to become polarized around these hot-button topics; thus the clinician's job is to assist families in exploring areas of conflict that naturally arise during this period and to adopt a nonjudgmental stance. The clinician can help provide a context for adolescence that may support families in normalizing the challenges that arise. For example, psychoeducation about brain development and executive functioning skills, the role of social relationships in identity formation and increasing need for a sense of independence are discussed to set the stage for Phase III. Parents may struggle with differentiating between normative exploration that supports identity development and pathologic or unsafe behaviors. Parents' own childhood, cultural background, religious beliefs and experience in raising teenagers contribute to the lens through which they view their child. The clinician's job is to help families reflect on their expectations and values as related to their child's return to healthy development. When there are conflicting views between family culture and expectations and those of the culture surrounding their child, the family is assisted in exploring the potential dilemmas they may face as they support their child in navigating these discrepancies.

Supervisory Intervention

In supervision, it may be useful to help guide and focus the discussion on common themes in adolescent development that individuals with EDs may exhibit struggles around. The clinician will also need to orient the family to typical phases of adolescent development. As in the manual, the teaching around development may be divided by stages: early (roughly age 12–14), middle (roughly age 14–16) and late (roughly age 16–19). Clinicians may begin by assessing family knowledge and expectations based on their own personal experiences to determine where they may need more instruction. The following guide can be utilized to support goal setting in Phase III— this is not an exhaustive list but rather represents more typical areas of focus in work with individuals with restrictive EDs. Remember that not all of these areas should or can be addressed, and in cases where skills deficits are pronounced, or are reflected in an unresolved comorbid mental health condition, the focus may be on highlighting the need for ongoing treatment in a different model (see foregoing discussion).

Phase III Treatment Planning Guide (Appendix X)

Theme	Typical development	Common challenges	Therapeutic interventions
Body image concerns	Body changes occur with puberty in early stages of adolescent development. Certain body image ideals are integrated based on feedback from one's sociocultural environment.	There are concerns about attractiveness and overemphasis on body image in self-worth Physical maturation is perceived as different than peers.	Provide psychoeducation on components of a healthy body and self-image. Build areas of self-worth outside of body image. Problem-solve triggers that maintain negative body image (e.g., wearing a bathing suit)

Theme	Typical development	Common challenges	Therapeutic interventions
		Physical maturation is a marker of increased independence that is cause for discomfort.	Encourage activities that broaden one's relationship with his/her body (e.g., focusing on health and utility rather than appearance). Address fears around emerging sexuality, increased responsibility and pressures and identify strategies to increase a sense of safety.
Communication	Independent voice is developing—teens begin to separate their views from those of their family and begin to consider alternative perspectives and practice communication of these with family and peers. Negotiation skills are learned and perspective taking, cognitive flexibility and other abstract-thinking skills continue to develop as adolescence progresses.	Difficulty expressing views in the context of social concerns/fear of judgment or making a social mistake Conflict avoidance Uncertainty in needs, wants and goals reflecting underlying emotion regulation challenges	Teach interpersonal effectiveness skills. Practice engaging family communication in areas of conflict with a focus on encouraging practice of basic communication skills (e.g., reflective listening, validation).
Managing the spectrum of impulsivity to inhibition	Typically adolescents are not able to employ complex executive functioning skills given brain maturational processes. Impulsive actions are typical with failure to think through consequences.	High impulsivity resulting in risk taking behaviors in multiple domains vs. High levels of inhibition and averseness to risk, leading to missed opportunities for growth and learning.	Orient families to typical vs. atypical/problematic levels of risk taking tailored to specific behavioral concerns. Help families set contingencies around problem behaviors. When the problem is inhibition, encourage families to create a supportive framework for novel experiences that may challenge and expand adolescent confidence around spontaneity/uncertainty.

(Continued)

(Continued)

Theme	Typical development	Common challenges	Therapeutic interventions
Difficulties in emotion regulation	Hormonal changes may intensify felt emotional experience. Adolescents may experience emotions as out of control or confusing and may have difficulty verbalizing emotions and using emotional data to effectively support decision making.	Maladaptive coping strategies to escape/ avoid aversive emotional states, resulting in a cycle of emotion dysregulation and lost opportunities to learn new skills to regulate emotions. Patients and families may see emotions as problematic/to be avoided.	Provide basic education on role of emotions/ model of emotion. Encourage families to reflect on their own beliefs and response to expressed emotion. Teach basic emotion regulation skills as needed.
Perfectionism/ low self-confidence	Adolescents seek feedback on their value/worth through peer comparisons. They can be overly sensitive to punishment (mistakes), less so to rewards, and may require assistance in incorporating these experiences into sense of self in a balanced and nonjudgmental fashion.	Unrealistically high standards may be reinforced through heightened attempts to succeed (overworking, hyper-attention to detail and relying on objective measures of success). Consequence of perfectionistic ideals is fear of mistakes, avoidance or hypervigilance and unending quest for achievement that is unrelenting and unfulfilled.	Assist families in exploring consequences of perfectionistic beliefs and behaviors. Encourage exposure framework to support management of perfectionistic behaviors and testing perfectionistic beliefs.

Within each of these areas of focus is an emphasis on social development—namely, helping teens navigate peer, family, adult and romantic relationships. Evidence suggests that interpersonal challenges are often present post-recovery from an ED (Lock, Couturier & Agras, 2006). Further, EDs often forestall development of healthy attachments as individuals typically become more socially isolated and are unable to participate for a time in typical social activities due to their illness. Thus, an adolescent with an ED is pulled toward the family at a time when they would otherwise be launching and it is the clinician's job to work with the family to hold this expectation moving forward. Families may themselves struggle with increased anxiety around allowing developmentally appropriate independence given their lived experience of a life-threatening illness. Further, other family members may also struggle with similar challenges as their child. Common areas of parent-child overlap in skills deficits include emotion dysregulation, cognitive inflexibility, conflict avoidance and high achievement orientation. All family members can benefit from a discussion of these important areas for skill development and the work of Phase III is framed within the context of the family system (e.g., the family is engaged in problem-solving and perspective-taking activities).

In supervision, it is often helpful to direct the clinician to think carefully about the family's response to their child's development and the way in which the ED brought their child more closely into the family fabric. Parental views and experience of autonomy versus dependence may be examined carefully to address any perceived barriers to their alignment with normative autonomy. In some cases, given the broad sweep of concerns that arise at this stage of development, guiding the clinician toward increased structure can be useful. We propose the following structure of sessions in Phase III:

1. Introduce the goals of Phase III with regards to normalizing adolescent development (review typical vs. atypical developmental patterns).
2. Review parents' expectations for development and impact of their own culture, values and upbringing.
3. Encourage parents to share their view of the impact of the ED on their child's development.
4. Assist the family in identifying skills deficits/areas of challenge that may have been vulnerabilities to the ED, or may present challenges in maintaining recovery (relapse prevention).
5. Provide input through review of the history of the ED and treatment to date on where the family sessions might focus, considering areas of overlap with parent goals.
6. Delineate a structure for addressing Phase III goals (may reference treatment planning tool).
7. Plan remaining sessions (1–2 to focus on area of concern, 1–2 to focus on termination).

Case Example: Extending Externalization as a Tool in Phase III

Externalization as it is introduced at the beginning of treatment should be used throughout to help parents gain clarity on areas of overlap and divergence in the realm of typical development, the ED and other areas of psychopathology. The case of Teresa provides an illustration of challenges parents may have in differentiating normative behavior from problem behavior in later stages.

The clinician arrived to supervision expressing bewilderment about how to respond to Teresa's mother's insistence that when Teresa began to whine, push back and get "willful" in response to her limit setting in normative areas of development, they were seeing a manifestation of her ED. Her response to Teresa's tendency to become emotionally labile and rejecting was to become increasingly vigilant around Teresa's eating, even though Teresa had been able to maintain a healthy weight with appropriate independence for a number of months. Upon further discussion, it was apparent that these behavioral patterns, while emerging for the first time in the context of the ED, were now serving to push back against normative parental limit setting, and reflected a deficit on the part of the adolescent in being able to regulate her own affective state and a strong desire to avoid negative emotion. In these instances, Teresa would elicit help from her parents and others in her environment, rather than practicing a more assertive communication style. These behaviors were tracked in supervision and the clinician was able to identify that they typically arose in contexts where Teresa experienced an emotional vulnerability threatening self-worth and self-confidence (e.g., in the context of peer rejection), and served to pull parents back into a supportive and protective role. Further, the supervisor encouraged the clinician to consider the potential consequences to the individual's development of keeping parents engaged in this way. Typically, when concerned, her mother would increase management of meals and snacks, and respond readily to her requests for additional support around basic needs. This kept Teresa from learning the skills to regulate her own emotional states such that she was not developing greater self-confidence and effective communication around her needs. When the clinician went back to the family with this observation, Teresa's mother experienced a sense of relief in "not having to go back to square 1" with the ED. This further highlighted the importance of another Phase III goal, which would be to assist the mother in developing a more sophisticated conceptualization and problem-solving skills around her daughter's range of behaviors. Further, the clinician recognized that the mother was still struggling with significant anxiety around the experience

*of her daughter's ED, leading to hypervigilance and misinterpreta-
tion of behavioral cues. In supervision, the clinician and supervisor identified interventions targeting the goals of increased emotion
identification, and highlighted communication challenges between
Teresa and her mother. Her mother learned to remain curious about
Teresa's behavior with her, reflecting observations back to Teresa
and prompting her to share her experience. This created space for
Teresa to reflect on her own emotional experience and communicate her needs more directly.*

How to Say Good-Bye: Managing Termination

Description of the Dilemma

It is not uncommon following therapy for clinicians and families to have difficulty saying good-bye. If a clinician has truly joined with a family, they will
have a unique therapeutic bond that reflects their collaborative journey in
overcoming the ED. Given the seriousness of the illness parents may express
a significant amount of gratitude toward the clinician. In some cases, families
may place undue responsibility for progress on the clinician's shoulders, and
in these situations, it is critical that the clinician refocus on empowering the
family. In fact, it would be expected that given the work around parental
empowerment throughout this treatment, families themselves may be able
to approach general challenges in their families with greater confidence in
their own skills. Reminding families of the tools they have developed over
the course of treatment and the flexibility with which these tools may be
applied to new challenges is an important element of the termination process. Indeed, the clinician's job in terminating is to also share her observations of the skills the family has brought to bear against the ED—the
strengths and qualities that both were inherent to the family and emerged in
the context of treatment.

Typically termination begins with a review of the treatment, which provides an opportunity for all to reflect on progress and ongoing points of
challenge. It is useful to frame this discussion in terms of the different phases
of treatment. It is not uncommon for families to revisit earlier emotions that
reflect their internalization of the seriousness of their child's illness and their
journey in helping them to overcome it. It is important to provide families
with space to reflect on their unique path in treatment, as their narrative
of this experience will be incorporated into their sense of self and sense of
family moving forward. Families often benefit from considering the ways in
which they have learned and changed in positive ways even in the midst of
a very challenging experience. The clinician may help guide this process by

asking families to reflect on what they have learned about themselves, the strengths they see in themselves and their family and how they would like to use this experience to shape future goals. The clinician may also share his or her own hopes for the young person and family moving forward.

Finally, clinicians provide psychoeducation on relapse prevention—for example, they help families to distinguish between lapses and full relapse, and encourage families to think through how they may respond to different signs of relapse once they have taken time to evaluate the seriousness of their concerns. Clinicians may revisit the Venn diagram, thereby reviewing the family's ability to distinguish between the eating disorder and more normative adolescent behavior. The family can be reminded to expect bumps in the road to recovery and are empowered to identify these and intervene quickly.

Supervisory Intervention

Supervision provides a parallel opportunity for clinicians to process their experience in working with the family and their reactions to the plan for termination. Saying good-bye is often more challenging when clinicians and families have formed a strong attachment. It is the supervisor's job to monitor for indications that the clinician is having a difficult time moving the termination process along at an appropriate rate. The supervisor can facilitate discussion around the challenges of termination by normalizing the range of experiences clinicians have in working with families. The following supervisory questions may help guide discussion and support identification of challenges the clinician is facing in terminating.

1. What markers of readiness are you using to determine a termination timeline?
2. When you consider terminating with this family, what is your reaction? Do you have particular concerns for this family?
3. What remaining hopes do you have for your work with the family? Are there goals that feel unmet? What capacity does the family have to manage these goals on their own?
4. Are there any indications that the family/young person would benefit from additional psychotherapy? What are your recommendations and why?
5. What barriers do you observe in yourself to saying good-bye to this family?

In FBT, it is often helpful to remind oneself that if we have successfully empowered families, they will ultimately feel ready to move forward independently, even when there are remaining unresolved challenges. The clinician has done his job when the family has a roadmap that allows them to approach future dilemmas successfully and extend their learning in treatment to novel situations. Spacing the sessions to a frequency of once per month in Phase III is a helpful practice in scaffolding, whereby a family is able to collect data about their capacity to approach difficulties without regular feedback from the clinician. When clinicians are reluctant to space sessions, or continue to expand focus to other areas when the aim is to move toward termination, the supervisor assists clinicians in reflecting on their own concerns or anxieties about letting a family conclude. Common concerns are often revealed through exploring the foregoing questions and include worry about unaddressed vulnerabilities to the ED (e.g., perfectionism, cognitive inflexibility, severe anxiety, conflict avoidance), unresolved comorbid conditions, the family's expressed desire for continued therapy and the clinician's fear of "abandoning" the family.

In all of these cases, the supervisor guides the clinician to bring these concerns into the open and share the observed dilemma back with the family. This opens the door for joint problem solving around anticipated challenges with ending treatment, and alternative solutions to continuing FBT (e.g., engaging in an alternative treatment, highlighting the ways in which parents can apply their learning to assist their child in working on other areas of skill-deficits, and encouraging parents to test their own fears about their ability to manage on their own). This also provides another opportunity for clinicians to reflect back family strengths and skills and remind them of the relapse prevention plan they have at their disposal, which can include a return meeting with the clinician for a booster session, a reevaluation if there is a relapse and/or access to other resources. We find that when families and clinicians engage in these conversations, the termination process is facilitated with less difficulty. Just as supervisors remind clinicians to reflect on their own ambivalence, the clinician normalizes ambivalent thoughts and emotions families have about termination.

References

Fitzpatrick, K. K. (2011). Developmental considerations when treating anorexia nervosa in adolescents and young adults. In J. Lock (Ed.), *The Oxford handbook of child and adolescent eating disorders: Developmental perspectives*. Oxford, UK: Oxford University Press.

Lock, J., Couturier, J., & Agras, W. S. (2006). Comparison of long-term outcomes in adolescents with anorexia nervosa treated with family therapy. *Journal of the American Academy of Child & Adolescent Psychiatry, 45*(6), 666–672.

10 Additional Considerations and Future Directions

Sarah Forsberg, James Lock and Daniel Le Grange

Additional Considerations

There are many challenges that arise when delivering FBT that are outside of the scope of this manual. However, we hope that the framework provided here—linking common dilemmas to solutions true to FBT principles and interventions, in the context of a clear supervisory structure—can be applied to many problems that have not been addressed here.

Some additional considerations that are worth mentioning relate to the question we hear frequently—under what circumstances is FBT contraindicated for an adolescent with an eating disorder (ED)? The evidence base for treatment of EDs in young patients is in its infancy when compared to other more common childhood psychiatric disorders. Therefore, our answer to this question is often unsatisfying in that we do not have any sophisticated algorithm to guide decisions about treatment assignment. That said, we often tell providers that the single clearest contraindication for engaging a family in FBT is when the caregivers themselves are well educated (are informed about what is required of them in this model, the risks, benefits and alternatives and existing empirical evidence), and yet decide to pursue an alternative path. At times, families are clear about their preferences at the outset, and others may attempt FBT and decide in the process that they lack the desire and resources to take on the task of renourishment. Even in these cases, we remind ourselves that families are resilient, can access newfound strength and skills in the midst of crisis, and with support can be buoyed by the clinician and treatment team as they develop their confidence in confronting their child's illness.

Most commonly we hear doubts about a family's abilities to carry out FBT by clinicians themselves when families have limited resources (e.g., may lack person-power in the case of single-parent or divorced families, may lack financial resources or social capital that allows for flexibility in scheduling or transportation, or may have their own mental health struggles). We briefly address some of these perceived barriers below with the aim of assisting clinicians in taking a flexible and open-minded approach to allow space for creative problem solving about whether to take up FBT with a particular family.

Unpacking Perceived Contraindications to FBT

Cultural Variables

Description of Dilemma

The dilemma here, as is the case in any treatment, is how to best deliver culturally competent treatment without compromising treatment integrity and potency. There are as yet no data on whether cultural background (including but not limited to ethnicity, race, religion and SES) impacts treatment engagement or outcome in FBT. Exploring these family variables is an important next step, especially given that EDs touch individuals from a diverse range of cultural backgrounds. However, the challenge herein is that limitations in research methodology coupled with sparse data will inevitably lack a lens toward intersectionality, the interrelated, transactional sociocultural identities that influence human experience. Across a broad-range of interventions for various clinical populations, ethnicity alone has not been found to be predictive of different outcomes. Further, there are mixed findings on the value of culturally tailored adaptations to evidence-based treatments (Huey, Tilley, Jones, & Smith, 2014). Such categorical approaches are unlikely to capture the nuances associated with cultural background that may have a more impactful relationship to treatment engagement and outcome. More recently published RCTs of FBT include families from diverse ethnic and racial backgrounds (around 25%). Race, ethnicity and SES have not been identified as predictors or moderators of treatment effects in any of these studies. However, sample sizes may be too small to detect differences, especially when further grouped by ethnic identity.

Supervisory Intervention

In an ongoing effort to uphold the highest standards of practice, supervisors and clinicians seek ongoing education on current best practices regarding cultural competency in the realm of psychotherapy. There are established guidelines that should be incorporated into the process of supervision (e.g., American Psychological Association Guidelines on Multicultural Education, Training, Research, Practice and Organizational Change for Psychologists, 2003; The American Psychiatric Association Best Practice Highlights for Treating Diverse Patient Populations, 2017).

A key tenet of FBT involves the clinician working toward *joining* families as a consultant. We believe keeping this tenet alive is akin to striving toward greater self- and human-awareness. Here, the clinician remains curious and open-minded, expresses respect for family values and preferences, and thereby seeks to simultaneously facilitate parental empowerment and the sense of being understood and respected by the clinician. How this is achieved will vary depending on the family's prior experiences, values and interactions with similar systems in concert with the clinician's own worldview derived from such experiences. In supervision, clinicians are encouraged to reflect on their own cultural background as it shapes their perceptions of and interventions with families. Supervisors strive to remain nonjudgmental in their efforts to assist clinicians in exploring their own biases and judgments, and model shared responsibility in unraveling these tensions. The supervisor also encourages the clinician to consider the culture from which FBT, like many other current behavioral therapies, was derived, and explore the impact of delivering a model that is inherently Eurocentric in its inception.

In supervision, the supervisor's task is to listen for any assumptions or judgments made by the clinician. As noted, it is helpful to normalize this process at the outset of supervision, highlighting the rationale for dissecting this shared human dilemma. In FBT, the following are common areas where we have seen judgments arise about a family's ability to engage in FBT:

- A family who has a limited reference point for mental health treatment. This might reflect experiencing environments where mental health issues are deeply stigmatized (e.g., may be seen as a weakness or a deep unresolvable flaw, or are blamed on families), are communicated and expressed differently (e.g., perhaps are expressed physically) or are treated using traditional medicinal practices not espoused by Western culture.
- A family who has experienced systematic oppression by those in position of authority, who may experience inherent difficulties in trusting authority.
- A family whose expectations for those in a position of authority do not align with a focus on creating a more egalitarian relationship.
- A family who has religious or cultural beliefs that delineate strong gender roles and norms for power/authority.
- A family who has limited social and economic capital that may limit their access to resources needed to support their child (e.g., food, shelter, transportation).
- A family who does not speak the dominant cultural language, who requires an interpreter.

In supervision, these cultural variances (among others) are explored with the aim of facilitating a greater awareness of the potential impact they may have on treatment. The supervisor and clinician determine how to best address these while simultaneously upholding the integrity of the approach.

Case Vignette

Amalia was a 15-year-old Mexican American girl with anorexia nervosa, who had moved in with her aunt and adult (19-year-old) cousin, following removal from her father's home. She had only

recently come to live with her aunt and cousin, whom she had posi-
tive relationships with, and her future living arrangement was uncer-
tain at the outset of treatment. In supervision, the first priority was
to assess whether Amalia's aunt was willing and able to engage in
FBT, as this had been the recommended approach following her
discharge from a medical hospitalization. Amalia's removal from her
father's home was prompted by multiple reports of physical abuse,
and thus while there was a pending investigation, the supervisor and
clinician both believed that it would be important for Amalia to be in
a stable living situation for FBT to be most efficacious. Thus, at the
outset, the clinician spent time thoroughly reviewing the structure
and process of FBT and the anticipated timeline and encouraged the
family to engage in problem solving around some of the challenges
they anticipated in taking responsibility for Amalia's treatment. The
family decided that they wanted to take on this role and the clini-
cian supported them in advocating with Amalia's case-worker for
the family to maintain guardianship at least for the duration of her
treatment. The other dilemma the supervisor assisted the clinician
with was determining how to best engage the family structure. While
Amalia's cousin was more like a sister to her, in their family struc-
ture, she also operated as a second adult figure. She held a full-
time job and she and her mother divided household responsibilities.
Given Amalia's aunt worked full-time as well, and they did not have
any other family nearby to support renourishment, the established
plan was for both adults to divide responsibility for meal planning,
preparation and supervision, depending on availability. From there,
the supervisor and clinician carefully monitored challenges associ-
ated with placing the cousin in an authoritative role. In this case,
Amalia was responsive to both family members' efforts. When her
ED was at its strongest, her caregivers would often call one another
for support to demonstrate their alignment and persistence. On the
weekends, Amalia and her cousin would plan outings that allowed
for connection outside of Amalia's illness and supported healthy
development.

Another complexity that arose in this case was that the aunt was monolin-
gual Spanish-speaking. This dilemma poses some additional questions about
how to best empower parents, and how to improve access to treatment when
resources like access to a trained interpreter are limited. Fortunately, in this

case, the clinician worked at an institution with access to an interpreter trained to work in a medical and mental health setting. Ahead we identify some practices we have found helpful in conducting therapy in the multi-lingual context.

While the clinician was able to access an interpreter for Amalia's family, the interpreters were not skilled in facilitating mental health treatment, and none had been historically involved in a full course of FBT. Not having worked with multilingual families historically the clinician initially suggested having Amalia's cousin serve as interpreter. The supervisor highlighted concerns about placing the cousin in this dual and conflicting role. For example, he noted that the cousin was not trained in interpretation, a highly skilled craft, might be biased in her report of what the mother was saying depending on her perspective and relationships within the family, and could put her in an uncomfortable position with her family members. She would unnaturally be one step removed from the family process, limiting her ability to stand in as co-parent in this particular family. Further, the supervisor had her read established ethical guidelines associated with the use of interpreters to further prepare her for this work. The supervisor then helped the clinician consider how to best prepare the interpreter for therapy sessions. First, they worked to identify a single interpreter who was regularly available during the allotted weekly therapy slot. The goal here was to ensure continuity and allow the clinician to train and prep the interpreter for the process. They took care to explain the therapy process to the interpreter, with specific attention to the nuances of FBT they felt would be most important to capture. These included a discussion of the importance of parental empowerment, externalization of illness, agnosticism, symptom focus, parental alignment and the role of siblings. The supervisor and clinician made a checklist of concepts and terms for the interpreter that were likely to arise in FBT. Further, they emphasized the importance of translating everything as it was spoken, and encouraged the interpreter to ask for a pause if there was any confusion.

During therapy, the clinician worked with the interpreter to determine the most helpful pacing of her communication, learning that she often spoke too fast. A review of videotaped sessions with the supervisor revealed that she also made eye contact with the interpreter, rather than family members. The supervisor encouraged her to attune to the family nonverbally (e.g., nodding, smiling, modulating eye contact, matching the family member's affect when appropriate). Even though she did not understand their verbal communication, she learned to observe nonverbal cues and express genuine interest through her own body language while the family spoke. Further, the supervisor and clinician identified additional strategies to aid in communication—they frequently created diagrams and lists and encouraged the family to summarize at the end of the session, which the interpreter then recorded for the family to take with them.

After each session, the clinician checked in with the interpreter to identify points of confusion, and potential emotional reactions the interpreter had to family content that arose during the session, allowing them to process and make necessary adjustments. Over time, the clinician and supervisor were able to identify patterns in family use of language that was thought to amplify power differentials. Specifically, Amalia frequently would turn away from her aunt to speak to her cousin in rapid English, which over time was framed as an attempt by the ED to divide mother and cousin when they were appropriately aligned (this more often than not occurred when mother was challenging the ED in some way). The clinician inquired about this hypothesis with the family and expressed concern about its impact on the family hierarchy. The aunt and cousin both shared the clinician's concern, and the clinician encouraged the cousin to respond in Spanish to facilitate inclusion of the mother.

As noted, not all settings have the luxury of a consistent interpreter. In these instances, the supervisor and clinician consider the risks/benefits of utilizing a more nonconventional approach versus referring to another provider who may be able to provide language-congruent care, but may not be well versed in the treatment of EDs, let alone FBT. An alternative to the gold standard of in-person interpretation is using a telephone interpreting service, for example. It is important for clinicians to recognize that even in the best of circumstances, there will be barriers to effective use of interpretation, and supervision is an ideal venue to remain attuned to these. Supervisors and clinician should seek out additional resources and guidelines in the event they need to utilize an interpreter (Searight & Searight, 2009).

Working With Divorced or Single-Parent Families

Another family cultural variable that can be a source of concern for providers as they embark on treating a family with FBT is when parents are divorced, or are single, such that they are the sole provider for their child. There is some data to suggest that young people with EDs whose families are not intact fare better in a longer duration of treatment, although these effects were not maintained over time (Lock, Agras, Bryson, & Kraemer, 2005).

These data suggest that clinicians consider the unique challenges faced by these families but do not provide justification for predicting whether a family can do FBT. Here again, we encourage supervisors and clinicians to turn to the family, provide them with thorough information about what can be expected in treatment and highlight the particular dilemmas other families in their position have faced. It is often helpful for a family to hear about other families who have struggled and overcome a similar predicament to know that this treatment can be done, even when facing understandable barriers (e.g., families who are in an acutely stressful phase of separation or divorce, parents who are highly conflictual, and even those who have difficulty aligning their co-parenting more broadly). Clinicians here encourage families to take a self-reflective stance in anticipating challenges unique to their situation. We provide general recommendations for families who are divorced/separated; however, these should be tailored to each family:

- We recommend that if possible, one parent be the primary person conducting renourishment, whereby the other parent engages in a wide range of other support activities. Parental roles and responsibilities are clearly delineated up front.
- In many cases, this means that previous arrangements with regards to physical custody may need to be put on hold to increase consistency and stability around mealtimes (and minimize the potential vulnerabilities associated with transitions).
- When parents are unable to modify their division of responsibility and physical custody for a brief time in the context of treatment, we recommend families identify a structure for effective communication so that each is abreast of adherence to the meal regimen decided upon, and any challenges therein.
- Parents are educated at the outset about their increased vulnerability (as for all parents of children with EDs) to being divided by the illness. The clinician notes that prior disagreements with regards to parenting and their relationship may serve as ammunition for the ED to pit one parent against another. Parents are asked to reflect on how they have managed this challenge in relation to other, less acute parenting dilemmas as a means of drawing out previously utilized skills (or to uncover skills deficits).
- Clinicians highlight the importance of putting other, unresolved conflicts temporarily on hold, while acknowledging the difficulty this poses. By amplifying the gravity of the child's illness, the clinician encourages parents to place their concerns in context of the immediate crisis.

Here, the clinician may use medical analogies to highlight the grave impact prioritizing other family conflicts may have on their child's health. "*If your 16-year-old was in a motorcycle accident and required several weeks of in-home traction, would you move the hospital bed back and forth between homes? If one home had a bathroom that was more accessible for a teenager in casts, wouldn't you use that home as opposed to the one with a tiny shower?*" These analogies are meant to emphasize the seriousness of the disorder that requires similar changes to other life-threatening medical or psychiatric issues.

When working with single-parent families, there is often real concern about whether the parent will be able to face the responsibility for the many tasks associated with renourishment. In these cases, it is helpful to obtain an overview of a family's range of psychosocial supports. Clinicians explore whether the parent has extended family members available to help or is a part of a supportive community that could be a resource (e.g., a church, neighborhood group, the school community). Some parents may be reluctant to draw on others for help, often due to concerns about posing a burden, or shame about their struggles, and the clinician seeks to address these.

Supervisory Intervention

Supervisors assist clinicians in using creative problem solving, which can then be integrated into family sessions. Supervisors are in a unique position to generate solutions based on prior experiences with single-parent families. Here are some ideas that families and clinicians have come up with in the past that have proved helpful in the absence of another parent:

- A grandparent living in the area or in the home takes over meal planning and preparation.
- Local relatives offer to provide meal support when a parent is unable to, or serve as backup respite. They are invited to attend treatment to become educated on the approach. Similarly, close family friends may be involved in this manner.
- A trusted person from school supervises snacks and lunches (e.g., school counselor, nurse, close teacher or administrator).
- A family with Medicare works with the county to receive wraparound services, whereby a behavioral health specialist provides meal support in the home and the FBT clinician provides training and consultation to align their efforts.
- A family hires a home-health aide.
- A family has meals delivered to the home to decrease the amount of time spent on meal preparation.
- Menus are written in advance and posted where family members can see, to accommodate changing schedules of supervision.
- The family's nanny or au pair joins sessions and implements some of the meals at home.
- The family is able to outsource other household tasks temporarily—they may have peripheral family or hired home aides help with cleaning and shopping, for example, to free parent time to focus on renourishment.
- Clinicians may support parents in accessing family medical leave, or provide letters to employers explaining the temporary and critical demands being placed on the parent to renourish their child.

Aligning Teams and Systems

Description of Dilemma

Differences in the orientation of the broader treatment team (as influenced by their training background, broader system and treatment philosophy) can influence the messages families receive about treatment. Ideally, medical providers, dieticians, psychiatrists and any other professional involved in caring for a child with an ED will have expertise in working with this population, and more so, be trained in the basic principles of FBT. Even in these cases, shared training experiences and philosophy can be trumped by broader systems issues, including limited resources, billing requirements, and the historical structure and function of different team members. When providers enter treatment with a family, they inevitably join a broader system with its own norms, strengths and limitations. Barriers to managing conflicting perspectives or practices include those that are practical (opportunities for communication are limited by scheduling or location) or personal (prior training, role definitions and individual preferences may impact alignment with FBT).

Supervisory Intervention

Guiding clinicians in managing systems and teams is an important function of an FBT supervisor. The supervisor is responsible for educating the new clinician about the current system, historical challenges faced in the process of team integration, and strategies that are required to successfully manage the system in the interest of providing consistent care. Taking on these tasks may be overwhelming for a new clinician who is a relative "outsider" to the system, is unfamiliar with the challenges, and may lack confidence in taking a leadership role with the broader team. It can be even more challenging working with outside providers, or across many systems (e.g., the clinician working in a private practice, coordinating with others in community-based settings and independent practice). We find that for families, receiving care in one setting can be a reassuring experience, especially for those who have had the unfortunate experience of hearing ten different perspectives and sets of recommendations from ten different providers. Therefore, depending on the context, clinicians may need to spend extra time and effort bringing all members of the team together. If this is not achieved early in treatment, families are likely to become derailed and clinicians may find themselves spending much of their time redirecting families rather than engaging them in productive treatment. Supervisors monitor these challenges with the clinician early in treatment. Simply asking the clinician to reflect on the following questions can help keep a focus on curtailing these challenges:

- Can you identify any areas in which the family is expressing confusion about how to proceed, their role or what to expect in treatment?
- If so, what is the origin of these points of confusion? Can they be traced back to conflicting messages delivered by the team?
- If so, what have you done to intervene, or where might you become stuck in your communication with the team/family?

When there are team members unfamiliar with FBT, the clinician works with the supervisor to determine how to best educate the team. This process of education will inevitably be impacted by the receptiveness of other team members to modifying their approach, time constraints and other systemic barriers. We often recommend sharing an article with physicians on the role of the pediatrician in FBT (Katzman, Peebles, Sawyer, Lock, & Le Grange, 2013). At the very least, clinicians should familiarize themselves with the article, and we provide a brief overview of guidelines put forth in this article here. Further, in the event that barriers to team alignment are pronounced and remain unresolved despite the clinician's best efforts, clinicians work to educate the family on the importance of having a collaborative team. They help parents explore the impact of receiving conflicting messages on their ability to stay focused and may help the family access an FBT-congruent provider.

The Role of the Pediatrician in FBT: Guidelines

Key concept	In practice
Pediatrician is a consultant to caregivers.	– Involves parents in all sessions and informs them of all medical updates (lab values, vital sign and weight progress)
	– Provides feedback to families to support their decision-making process
	– Does not direct care unless there is a clear safety issue (e.g., patient needs hospitalization)
	– Seeks to build upon parental strengths and amplify parental confidence
	– Does not involve the adolescent in decision making until later phases, and in discussion with the family/clinician
Pediatrician is a consultant to the clinician.	– Provides medical updates to the clinician
	– Clinician communicates current treatment goals, progress and challenges back to the pediatrician
	– Works with the clinician and other team members to identify healthy weight targets prior to discussing with families
Pediatrician externalizes the illness to decrease family shame/guilt.	– Refers to the ED as separate from the patient and encourages the parents to do so as well
	– Remains agnostic about the cause of the ED
	– Normalizes struggles
Pediatrician and clinician strive for alignment.	– Does not make recommendations for therapy, yet shares thoughts and concerns with the clinician
	– Sets consistent goals with the clinician for recovery

Another system that may need to be utilized in treatment is the hospital setting when medically necessary. We recommend that hospitalization be utilized only when there is clear medical justification (e.g., there are serious vital sign abnormalities, lab abnormalities, extreme weight loss or severe food refusal), and that these are brief and focused on reversal of medical insta-bility. Even when hospitalizations are utilized for this purpose, supervisors and clinicians are aware of the potential for families to receive conflicting recommendations in these settings, and to potentially experience disempowerment by virtue of diffusion of responsibility, or destabilization of parental authority. Thus, supervisors will also support clinicians to take a leadership role in communicating with the hospital team about the family background, the treatment approach, and recommendations for care. Further, they will coach parents to be active participants in their child's treatment while they remain hospitalized.

Future Directions

There is much work to be done to enhance the efficacy of FBT, not limited to assisting supervisors and clinicians in practicing with greater fidelity. Many questions remain about when to recommend alternative approaches (as outlined earlier), what clinical populations can benefit, whether there are circumstances under which the approach should be adapted, and at what point there is clinical justification to shift to a different approach. Efforts are being made to explore the effectiveness of FBT in real-world clinical practice (Accurso, Fitzsimmons-Craft, Ciao, & Le Grange, 2015), where authors found comparable outcomes in rate of weight gain for those starting treatment at relatively higher body weights as those enrolled in an RCT. This is a first step in addressing concern that FBT is not translatable to broader clinical contexts.

Despite being the first-line treatment for adolescent EDs, a substantial number of patients do not improve with treatment. Thus, efforts are underway to develop a stepped-care model designed around benchmarks of progress, specifically early weight gain, to explore the efficacy of variants in the structure of therapy (a separated versus conjoint family approach) (Le Grange et al., 2016) and to add targeted adaptations for those who do not make early progress. Others are exploring the utility of adaptations for transition-age youth (TAY) (e.g., ages 19–25), who may still be largely reliant on family support (Dimitropoulos et al., 2015), and how to best benchmark weight progress in those with atypical AN (Hughes, Le Grange, Court, & Sawyer, 2017). Additionally FBT is manualized for adolescents with BN (Le Grange & Lock, 2009), and evidence from an RCT suggests those receiving FBT had higher rates of abstinence from binge/purge behaviors than those in cognitive-behavioral therapy (Le Grange, Lock, Agras, Bryson, & Jo, 2015). There are currently pilot projects underway exploring its utility with individuals with avoidant/restrictive food intake disorder (ARFID), and clinical adaptations have been outlined (Fitzpatrick, Forsberg, & Colborn, 2015). Finally, increasing efforts to explore the utility of technology-assisted intervention to expand access to care include delivery of FBT via telehealth, and an online, guided self-help platform (Anderson, Byrne, Crosby, & Le Grange, 2017; Lock, Darcy, Fitzpatrick, Vierhile, & Sadeh-Sharvit, 2017). Both of these pilot studies had promising outcomes, suggesting that FBT may be effectively delivered in varied formats.

Here, we elaborate on current efforts exploring the utility of parent-focused treatment (PFT), adaptations for poor early weight gain and FBT with TAY.

Using a Separated Family Format: Parent-Focused Treatment

Historically, FBT has been delivered in both a separated and conjoint format, based upon early work on the role of expressed emotion (EE) in family therapy (Eisler, Simic, Russell, & Dare, 2007; Le Grange, Eisler, Dare, & Hodes, 1992; Le Grange, Hoste, Lock, & Bryson, 2011). Data suggests that families who are highly critical, directing hostility toward their child, may fare better in a separated format (Eisler et al., 2000; Le Grange et al., 1992). A recent RCT explored differences in treatment outcome between conjoint FBT and a separated model, or parent-focused treatment (PFT). In PFT, the adolescent was not seen by the clinician, and instead was weighed by a skilled nurse prior to the parent session. The nurse met with the patient for 15 minutes, shared the weight and provided brief supportive counseling. The findings point to equally efficacious outcomes across the two treatments by the one-year follow-up point; however, PFT was superior in bringing about full remission by the end of treatment (Le Grange et al., 2016). Future research on potential moderators of treatment outcome may eventually help with treatment assignment.

Description of the Dilemma

As of yet, there is not a guidepost for clinicians to turn to when deciding whether to recommend a family try separated versus conjoint FBT. The following guideline may help clinicians and families decide upon a format, keeping data on EE in mind.

Supervisory Intervention

At this juncture, we recommend supervisors and clinicians engage in one of the following processes to guide decision making about the structure of treatment.

1. Present the family with treatment options and the evidence base and help the family think through some of the pros and cons of each format. For example, potential benefits of conjoint FBT are that it:

    *   Allows the clinician to observe family communication and to intervene as necessary (e.g., to help parents practice externalization in the session, to redirect criticism, to observe where parents struggle to set limits around illness-related behavior).

- Allows the clinician to model distress tolerance and containment, to bring the ED to the forefront in a way that allows parents to better understand their child's internal struggle.
- Allows the clinician to model warmth and limit setting simultaneously.
- May support the development of positive sibling relationships.
- May help adolescents access their healthy voice and over time their understanding and appreciation of their parents' interventions.
- Patients may increasingly participate in healthy ways that guide treatment decision making.

Potential challenges of conjoint FBT are as follows:

- Given the difficulties that arise in the renourishment process early in treatment, parents may express frustration and direct criticism at their child, or at the treatment model. Patients may feel blamed, feel like a burden and argue alongside parents against the approach.
- Parents may be reluctant to bring up some sensitive topics in front of their children that directly impact treatment.
- Families who are more conflict-avoidant may refrain from openly expressing thoughts/feelings because of concern about inciting distress.
- The ED may use these sessions as an opportunity to thwart parental efforts. Some individuals may become so disruptive in session that it is difficult for parents to mobilize around renourishment efforts (e.g., adolescents may refuse to engage in any way in the process, may interrupt, scream and yell, sob, threaten self-harm, run away, attempt to engage parents and the clinician in other seemingly important topics that distract from the symptom focus—e.g., struggles with peers, self-esteem issues).

2.   The clinician provides a treatment recommendation based on his or her clinical observations.

   Following a family assessment, the supervisor engages clinicians in a discussion of observations of family communication, exploring indicators of high levels of criticism. They identify whether there are family structural issues, or parental issues that pose a significant roadblock to engaging the full family in sessions. For example, such situations might include parents who are in the middle of a separation or divorce and are requesting extra support around navigating this process while finding common ground in renourishment. Or, parents may share their own mental health struggles that may impact their engagement (e.g., parents with an active ED would like to openly discuss their own challenges as they relate to their efforts at renourishment without negatively impacting their child; or a parent who was a victim of childhood abuse in their family of origin who experiences reactivation of early trauma when their child's ED becomes hostile and physical). While these dilemmas are not automatic exclusion criteria for participating in conjoint FBT, they warrant consideration in deciding the structure of treatment. Oftentimes, these are the types of issues that arise *during* treatment and when they do, supervision will involve careful deliberation about whether they justify a shift in the treatment framework. Placing these challenges in the context of treatment progress overall (e.g., are these thought to be distracting from the renourishment process, has progress been slow or nonexistent despite many weeks of treatment, are parents consistently requesting a change in format?) will help guide decision making.

Applying FBT to Transition-Age Youth

Description of the Dilemma

While RCTs of FBT have focused on adolescents aged 12–18, in clinical practice providers are using the approach with transition-age youth (TAY). FBT has higher success rates when applied to younger patients, underscoring the need for developmental considerations as applied to TAY. In practice, clinicians interviewed as a part of a qualitative study highlight a sensitivity to the developmental need for increasing autonomy in this group. In many cases, conducting FBT represented a significant step backward in development when individuals had launched into an independent lifestyle. Parents and patients alike may thus be initially more reluctant to engage in FBT. Generally, clinicians reported taking a more collaborative stance with TAY given both the need for explicit consent to involve parents and, in many cases, a greater willingness and ability to provide insight into their own struggles. All clinicians reported extending individual time with the patient, modifying their approach to externalization by providing more insight-oriented examples of the way in which the ED had interfered with life values and goals. In Phase III, clinicians reported spending more time with the TAY on relapse prevention and planning ahead for future challenges to support their successful transition to greater autonomy (Dimitropoulos et al., 2015).

Supervisory Intervention

While there is much to learn about how to best adapt FBT for the TAY population, some general guidelines for discussion in supervision may be useful here. First, the supervisor and clinician must decide whether an individual patient is appropriate for FBT. The following questions may guide this determination:

- Does the patient live with caregivers or are they easily accessible?
  - If there are barriers to including parents, the individual's support people may be more broadly defined and include partners, close friends and other adult family members.

- Is the patient willing to have parents involved?

  - An individual age 18 and over in many Western countries is required to provide consent to treatment. Once initial consent is obtained, the clinician and patient continue to engage in regular conversations about the type of information that is shared. The clinician invites the patient to share concerns about disclosures as they arise.
  - It is expected that TAY will experience wavering levels of ambivalence, which should be normalized and addressed in individual sessions.

- Are parents or other support people able and willing to be involved?

  - Clinicians and patients may need to engage in creative problem solving when an individual does not live with his or her support system. For example, use of technology, like videoconferencing systems, to allow for shared meals may be useful.
  - TAY may be provided with more opportunities for early practice with independent eating as dictated by both availability of the support system and their preferences. Simultaneously, at the outset of treatment, clinicians are transparent about the potential risks involved (especially when there is a high degree of medical acuity) when attempting renourishment without support.

The informed consent process may require more time with TAY and their support systems and should highlight some of the requirements listed earlier, as well as education about the important ways in which FBT is modified:

- The clinician emphasizes the importance of a collaborative relationship with both parents and patient, and highlights where this may be challenging (e.g., an individual may become unwilling at some point to have parents intervene around dangerous ED behaviors).
- The clinician highlights the gravity of restrictive EDs and potential long-term consequences and ensures that these match and amplify the concerns of the patient (e.g., the clinician might highlight the incredible importance of developing autonomy with regards to patient-specific goals).
- The clinician normalizes the natural tension patients and their support systems face in reverting to earlier stages of development. At the same time, the clinician stresses the gravity of the illness, lack of effective treatments for adults with AN, and the temporary nature of the arrangement.
- The clinician explores the patient's level of motivation, seeking to amplify healthy aspects of the self, and takes great care to reinforce healthy goals and choices.

Intensive Parent Coaching (IPC) for Early Non-Responders

Description of Dilemma

There is a significant need to identify adaptations to FBT to improve outcomes for those who do not achieve full remission at EOT (50%–65% in existing RCTs). To date, the most consistent early prognostic indicator is early weight gain (4–5 pounds) in the first four sessions. Those who do not reach this benchmark are unlikely to remit by the end of treatment (Doyle, Le Grange, Loeb, Doyle, & Crosby, 2010; Le Grange, Accurso, Lock, Agras, & Bryson, 2014). A recent feasibility study explored the addition of three intensive parent coaching (IPC) sessions, targeting parental self-efficacy, alignment and refinement of parental renourishment skills. Those patients requiring the adaptation ultimately had a comparable rate of recovery to those who met weight gain criteria (rates of full remission were 58% and 63% respectively) (Lock et al., 2015).

Supervisory Intervention

In supervision, it may be helpful to review the existing data supporting these adaptations. Here, we provide a brief description of the three additional sessions that were added when patients did not gain 4.8 lbs. by Session 4.

Session 4: The clinician focuses on reorchestrating a grave scene, as described in Session 1. Families are informed of the importance of early weight gain, and the clinician revisits the patient's trajectory in treatment, highlighting points of progress, while working to reinvigorate parental efforts to optimize their child's chances of full recovery. Here, the clinician emphasizes and amplifies specific family concerns for the impact the ED is having on their child. Clinicians emphasize the incredible challenge posed by AN, joining the family in observing the ways in which the illness had thwarted their efforts. Caution is taken to promote a sense of mobilization and hopefulness; therefore redirection of criticism is also an important intervention.

Session 5: This is a parent-only session, whereby the clinician prepares a formulation about the specific challenges the family faces in renourishing their child. Clinicians review 1–3 specific areas they feel the family would benefit from focusing on over the upcoming week. Common themes include addressing marital discord, problems in parent communication, conflict avoidance (fear of invoking distress) and difficulties with emotion regulation. The clinician determines whether parents need additional skills and directs them to appropriate resources.

Session 6: The final and subsequent adapted session is another family meal, the difference here being that parents are asked to bring a meal that they feel would be particularly challenging to their child's illness.

During the meal, the therapist assists the family in identifying changes they made following the first family meal and ongoing struggles, and works with the family on refining and expanding their current skillset.

While data here is preliminary, the consistent evidence on the importance of early weight gain may prompt supervisors and clinicians to consider invoking these adaptations for families who do not make early progress. An RCT is currently underway testing the efficacy of IPC for early non-responders, in hopes that further evidence will support these interventions.

Concluding Comments

These are only a few of the important areas of inquiry that we hope will provide future guidance around best practice in the implementation of FBT. Over the past decade, the evidence base for FBT has grown significantly, making it the first-line treatment for adolescent AN (Le Grange et al., 2011; Le Grange & Lock, 2012; Lock et al., 2010; Lock, La Via, American Academy of Child and Adolescent Psychiatry Committee on Quality Issues, 2015; National Institute for Health and Care Excellence, 2017). Further, there have been significant and successful efforts to disseminate the model outside the academic institutions in which it was developed (Couturier et al., 2014; Hughes et al., 2014; Madden et al., 2015). Yet the need-service gap remains significant even with these efforts, and access to treatment is limited given the significant resources required to train to the highest level of competence. We hope this manual provides a useful tool for supervisors and clinicians alike who wish to delve deeper into the intricacies of practice of FBT. We encourage providers to make use of the available evidence base, return to the key tenets of FBT and utilize resources here to inspire a practice with a high degree of integrity.

References

Accurso, E. C., Fitzsimmons-Craft, E. E., Ciao, A. C., & Le Grange, D. (2015). From efficacy to effectiveness: Comparing outcomes for youth with anorexia nervosa treated in research trials versus clinical care. *Behaviour Research and Therapy, 65*, 36–41.

American Psychiatric Association. (2017). *Best practice highlights for treating diverse patient populations: A guide to help assessment and treatment of patients from diverse populations.* Retrieved from www.psychiatry.org/psychiatrists/cultural-competency/treating-diverse-patient-populations.

American Psychological Association. (2003). Guidelines on multicultural education, training, research, practice, and organizational change for psychologists. *American Psychologist, 58*(5), 377–402.

Anderson, K., Byrne, C., Crosby, R., & Le Grange, D. (2017). Utilizing telehealth to deliver family-based treatment for adolescent anorexia nervosa. *International Journal of Eating Disorders, 50*(10), 1235–1238.

Couturier, J., Kimber, M., Jack, S., Niccols, A., Van Blyderveen, S., & McVey, G. (2014). Using a knowledge transfer framework to identify factors facilitating implementation of family-based treatment. *International Journal of Eating Disorders, 47*(4), 410–417.

Dimitropoulos, G., Freeman, V. E., Allemang, B., Couturier, J., McVey, G., Lock, J., & Le Grange, D. (2015). Family-based treatment with transition age youth with anorexia nervosa: A qualitative summary of application in clinical practice, *Journal of Eating Disorders, 3*(1), 1–13.

Doyle, P. M., Le Grange, D., Loeb, K., Doyle, A. C., & Crosby, R. D. (2010). Early response to family-based treatment for adolescent anorexia nervosa. *International Journal of Eating Disorders, 43*(7), 659–662.

Eisler, I., Dare, C., Hodes, M., Russell, G., Dodge, E., & Le Grange, D. (2000). Family therapy for adolescent anorexia nervosa: The results of a controlled comparison of two family interventions. *Journal of Child Psychology and Psychiatry, 41*(6), 727–736.

Eisler, I., Simic, M., Russell, G. F. M., & Dare, C. (2007). A randomised controlled treatment trial of two forms of family therapy in adolescent anorexia nervosa: A five-year follow-up. *Journal of Child Psychology and Psychiatry, 48*(6), 552–560.

Fitzpatrick, K. K., Forsberg, S. E., & Colborn, D. (2015). Family-based therapy for avoidant restrictive food intake disorder: Families facing food neophobias. In K. Loeb, D. Le Grange, & J. Lock (Eds.), *Family therapy for adolescent eating and weight disorders: New applications* (pp. 256–276). New York: Routledge.

Huey, S. J., Tilley, J. L., Jones, E. O., & Smith, C. A. (2014). The contribution of cultural competence to evidence-based care for ethnically diverse populations. *Annual Review of Clinical Psychology, 10*, 305–338.

Hughes, E. K., Le Grange, D., Court, A., & Sawyer, S. M. (2017). A case series of family-based treatment for adolescents with atypical anorexia nervosa. *International Journal of Eating Disorders, 50*(4), 424–432.

Hughes, E. K., Le Grange, D., Court, A., Yeo, M., Campbell, S., Whitelaw, M., . . . Sawyer, S. M. (2014). Implementation of family-based treatment for adolescents with anorexia nervosa. *Journal of Pediatric Health Care, 28*(4), 322–330.

Katzman, D. K., Peebles, R., Sawyer, S. M., Lock, J., & Le Grange, D. (2013). The role of the pediatrician in family-based treatment for adolescent eating disorders: Opportunities and challenges. *The Journal of Adolescent Health, 53*(4), 433–440.

Le Grange, D., Accurso, E. C., Lock, J., Agras, S., & Bryson, S. W. (2014). Early weight gain predicts outcome in two treatments for adolescent anorexia Nervosa. *International Journal of Eating Disorders, 47*(2), 124–129.

Le Grange, D., Eisler, I., Dare, C., & Hodes, M. (1992). Family criticism and self-starvation: A study of expressed emotion. *Journal of Family Therapy, 14*(2), 177–192.

Le Grange, D., Hoste, R. R., Lock, J., & Bryson, S. W. (2011). Parental expressed emotion of adolescents with anorexia nervosa: Outcome in family-based treatment. *International Journal of Eating Disorders, 44*(8), 731–734.

Le Grange, D., Hughes, E. K., Court, A., Yeo, M., Crosby, R. D., & Sawyer, S. M. (2016). Randomized clinical trial of parent-focused treatment and family-based treatment for adolescent anorexia nervosa. *Journal of the American Academy of Child & Adolescent Psychiatry, 55*(8), 683–692.

Le Grange, D., & Lock, J. (2009). *Treating bulimia nervosa in adolescents: A family based approach* (1st ed.). New York: Guilford Press.

Le Grange, D., Lock, J., Agras, W. S., Bryson, S. W., & Jo, B. (2015). Randomized clinical trial of family-based treatment and cognitive-behavioral therapy for adolescent bulimia nervosa. *Journal of the American Academy of Child & Adolescent Psychiatry, 54*(11), 886–894.

Lock, J., Agras, W. S., Bryson, S., & Kraemer, H. C. (2005). A comparison of short- and long-term family therapy for adolescent anorexia nervosa. *Journal of the American Academy of Child & Adolescent Psychiatry, 44*(7), 632–639.

Lock, J., Darcy, A., Fitzpatrick, K. K., Vierhile, M., & Sadeh-Sharvit, S. (2017). Parental guided self-help family based treatment for adolescents with anorexia nervosa: A feasibility study. *International Journal of Eating Disorders, 50*(1), 1104–1108.

Lock, J., La Via, M., & American Academy of Child and Adolescent Psychiatry (AACAP) Committee on Quality Issues (CQI). (2015). Practice parameter for the assessment and treatment of children and adolescents with eating disorders. *Journal of the American Academy of Child & Adolescent Psychiatry, 54*(5), 412–425.

Lock, J., Le Grange, D., Agras, W. S., Fitzpatrick, K. K., Jo, B., Accurso, E., . . . & Stainer, M. (2015). Can adaptive treatment improve outcomes in family-based therapy for adolescents with anorexia nervosa? Feasibility and treatment effects of a multi-site treatment study. *Behaviour Research and Therapy, 73*, 90–95.

Lock, J., Le Grange, D., Agras, W. S., Moye, A., Bryson, S. W., & Jo, B. (2010). Randomized clinical trial comparing family-based treatment with adolescent-focused individual therapy for adolescents with anorexia nervosa. *Archives of General Psychiatry, 67*(10), 1025.

Madden, S., Miskovic-Wheatley, J., Wallis, A., Kohn, M., Lock, J., Le Grange, D., . . . Touyz, S. (2015). A randomized controlled trial of in-patient treatment for anorexia nervosa in medically unstable adolescents. *Psychological Medicine, 45*(2), 415–427.

National Institute for Health and Care Excellence. (2017). *Eating disorders: Recognition and treatment.* Retrieved from: https://www.nice.org.uk/guidance/ng69/resources/eating-disorders-recognition-and-treatment-pdf-1837582159813

Rienecke, R. D., Accurso, E. C., Lock, J., & Le Grange, D. (2016). Expressed emotion, family functioning, and treatment outcome for adolescents with anorexia nervosa. *European Eating Disorders Review, 24*(1), 43–51.

Searight, H. R., & Searight, B. K. (2009). Working with foreign language interpreters: Recommendations for psychological practice. *Professional Psychology: Research and Practice, 40*(5), 444–451.

Appendices

Appendix I: List of Recommended Readings

Seminal Texts

Le Grange, D., & Lock, J. (Eds.). (2011). *Children and adolescents with eating disorders: Handbook of assessment and treatment.* New York: Guilford Press.

Lock, J., & Le Grange, D. (2005). *Help your teenager beat an eating disorder.* New York: Guilford Press.

Lock, J., & Le Grange, D. (2013). *Treatment manual for anorexia nervosa: A family-based approach* (2nd ed.). New York: Guilford Press.

Position Papers

Le Grange, D., Lock, J., Loeb, K., & Nicholls, D (2010). An academy for eating disorders position paper: The role of the family in eating disorders. *International Journal of Eating Disorders, 43*(1), 1–5.

Lock, J., La Via, M. C., & American Academy of Child and Adolescent Psychiatry (AACAP) Committee on Quality Issues (CQI). (2015). Practice parameter for the assessment and treatment of children and adolescents with eating disorders *Journal of the American Academy of Child and Adolescent Eating Disorders, 54*(5), 412–425.

Katzman, D., Peebles, R., Sawyer, M., Lock, J., & Le Grange, D. (2013). The role of the pediatrician in family-based treatment for adolescent eating disorders: Opportunities and challenges. *Journal of Adolescent Health, 53*(4), 433–440.

Research Articles

Agras, W. S., Lock, J., Brandt, H., Bryson, S. W., Dodge, E., Halmi, K., . . . Woodside, B. (2014). Comparison of two family therapies for adolescent anorexia nervosa: A randomized parallel trial. *JAMA Psychiatry, 71*(11), 1279–1286.

Le Grange, D., Accurso, E., Lock, J., Agras, W. S., & Bryson, S. W. (2014). Early weight gain in treatment predicts outcome in two treatments for adolescent anorexia nervosa. *International Journal of Eating Disorders, 47*(2), 124–129.

Le Grange, D., Hughes, E., Court, A., Yeo, M., Crosby, R., & Sawyer, S. (2016). Randomized clinical trial of parent-focused treatment and family-based treatment for adolescent anorexia nervosa. *Journal of the American Academy of Child and Adolescent Psychiatry, 55*(8), 683–692.

Le Grange, D., Lock, J., Accurso, E., Agras, S., Darcy, A., Forsberg, S., & Bryson, S. (2014). Relapse from remission at four-year follow-up in two treatments for adolescent anorexia nervosa. *Journal of the American Academy for Child and Adolescent Psychiatry, 53*(11), 1162–1167.

Le Grange, D., Lock, J., Agras, W. S., Moye, A., Bryson, S., Jo, B., & Kraemer, H. (2012). Moderators and mediators of remission in family-based treatment and adolescent focused therapy for anorexia nervosa. *Behavior Research and Therapy, 50*(2), 85–92.

Lock, J., Agras, S., Bryson, S., & Kraemer, H. (2005). A comparison of short- and long-term family therapy for adolescent anorexia nervosa. *Journal of the American Academy of Child and Adolescent Psychiatry, 44*(7), 632–639.

Lock, J., Couturier, J., & Agras, W. S. (2006). Comparison of long-term outcomes in adolescents with anorexia nervosa treated with family therapy. *Journal of the American Academy of Child and Adolescent Psychiatry, 45*(6), 666–672.

Lock, J., Le Grange, D., Agras, S., Bryson, S., & Jo, B. (2010). Randomized clinical trial comparing family-based treatment to adolescent focused individual therapy for adolescents with anorexia nervosa. *Archives of General Psychiatry, 67*(10), 1025–1032.

Lock, J., Le Grange, D., Agras, S., Fitzpatrick, K., Jo, B., Accurso, E., ... Stainer, M. (2015). Can adaptive treatment improve outcomes in family-based therapy for adolescents with anorexia nervosa? Feasibility and treatment effects of a multi-site treatment study. *Behaviour Research and Therapy, 73*, 90–95.

Sawyer, S. M., Whitelaw, M., Le Grange, D., Yeo, M., & Hughes, E. K. (2016). Physical and psychological morbidity in adolescents with a typical anorexia nervosa. *Pediatrics, 137*(4).

Appendix II: Supervisee Needs Assessment

1. Tell me about your prior training background. Have you worked with eating disorder populations? In what capacity? Do you have any prior training or exposure to FBT? In what setting?

2. What interests do you have in learning FBT? In working with families? In working with individuals with eating disorders?

3. What other treatment models/theoretical orientations have you received training in?

4. Have you done any previous treatment with families? Couples?

5. What do you hope to achieve in completing training in FBT? How do you see this experience fitting with your training and career goals?

6. What do you feel are your strengths as a clinician and areas for growth?

Appendix III: Case Presentation Guide for FBT

Family and adolescent presenting information	
Name	
Age	
Family constitution (who is in the family, who attends sessions, relevant background)	
Summary of eating disorder history	
Duration of illness	
Current height/weight/BMI percentile	
Weight history (data from growth curve)	
Previous treatment history, including comorbid conditions	
Hypotheses on family maintaining behaviors (e.g., imbalance in family structure, parental conflict around approach, beliefs about the illness that inform intervention)	

Appendix IV: Supervision Tracking Form

Supervision date:

Current session # and phase:

Weight progress:

Any significant safety issues needing immediate attention? Ethical dilemmas?

How was the session structured—what FBT-specific interventions occurred? Did any not occur that should have? Why?

Family barriers and strengths:

Supervision questions and related training/competency issues:

Appendix V: Fidelity Coding Framework: Session 1 The below scale for sessions 1, 2 and remaining phase III sessions rates effectiveness of therapist interventions on a scale of 1 (not at all effective) to 7 (very effective) in their delivery. Descriptive benchmarks are provided to help guide ratings and self-reflection. The same principles apply to patients with restrictive EDs aside from anorexia (AN). Note that descriptives are not provided for all rating levels.

Rating codes	Examples and illustrations*
Greeting family in sincere but grave manner: this taps into communicating the severity and immediacy of AN, as well as style of communication; a primary goal here is to match and shape the family emotion toward a more serious, problem-focused state.	1 = Therapist presents with a bubbly or joking demeanor; smiling or overly soothing; therapist harsh or cold; therapist affect incongruent 2 = 3 = Therapist response does not shape that of family or content; neutral demeanor; therapist may respond inappropriately to tenor of family emotions; may convey seriousness without empathy (or vice versa); hesitant style 4 = Generally conveys both severity and warmth, but affective tone is variable or unbalanced at times or the therapist may have difficulty with pacing the session (taking in all the concerns of the family) 5 = Therapist drives or shapes emotional tenor of the session; warm and empathic but firm and focused; good pacing of the session to build the tension of the session 6 = Unhesitating and straightforward, directs session well; good use of building momentum and maintaining focus 7 = Quiet, confident, competent demeanor; therapist "occupies space" well in the context of the therapy session and manages concerns with knowledge; warm and empathic in delivery of all messages, but continues to be firm in delivery of strong or difficult ideas
Engaging each family member: therapist asks each family member for introductions; evaluation of relationships between family members; engages each family member in gathering information throughout the session.	1 = Boring, not engaging, ignoring behaviors, or hyperfocus on one or two family members (esp. if caught up in conflict between a dyad); exclusionary or distant; heavily engages in unhealthy discussion with patient 2 = More focus on the patient or sibling; greater use of direct rather than circular questioning 3 = Attempts to gather information but ignores certain family members or engages with unhealthy part of the patient; may move on before providing appropriate opportunities for each family member to contribute to history; some use of direct and circular questioning; efforts at rapport building are unbalanced across family members

Rating codes	Examples and illustrations*
	4 = Attempts to engage each member either directly or with circular questioning; efforts to engage patient are present, but pursued further only if engaging with "healthy part" of the patient; gathers some history from family that supports relationship; solid effort at rapport building
	5 =
	6 = Gathers information about facts as well as relationships; good balance of questions and a smooth flow of questions of different family members; clear attempts to understand and connect with family members and use of circular questioning to understand relationships between members
	7 = Focused questioning; engages each member and gathers information; actively engaged and interested; strong efforts to develop rapport or alliance with each family member
Take a history focused on AN: therapist focuses on AN, including development of the disorder, current behaviors and impact on social/cognitive and familial relationships.	1 = Therapist engages in discussion about factors unrelated to the ED without bringing the focus back; pontificating or educating that interferes with obtaining information; judgmental approach to concerns raised or steps taken by parents
	2 = Asks questions without context or in a haphazard fashion; hyperfocus on specific details rather than a cohesive story
	3 = Spends undue time gathering history such that the focus moves away from building the momentum of the session
	4 = Gathers information on symptoms (restriction, binge/purge, exercise); development of the disorder and when family became concerned and steps taken to address these behaviors; gathers both past and present information about ED; missing information on the breadth of impact of disorder
	5 =
	6 =
	7 = Gathers info about the impact of AN from all family members; evaluates all domains (social, cognitive, emotional and impact in multiple domains) as well as symptoms at multiple time points (i.e., initial development and current presentation)
Externalization of illness: for Session 1 this must include teaching externalization to the family	1 = Passive therapist; failure to respond to most opportunities to shape or reinforce externalization
	2 = May use externalizing statements in a vague or general manner
	3 = Does not directly teach externalization but may use the language of externalization ("That is the illness"); may use the family's language or experience

(*Continued*)

Rating codes	Examples and illustrations*
	4 = Therapist introduces/teaches externalization and expands or reinforces this in session once or twice; uses a metaphor to externalize
	5 = Greater use of opportunities to help the family externalize; more active therapist
	6 = Greater use of doing so in a way that reflects the family's language or experiences
	7 = Therapist uses the family's language and issues to reshape or reinforce externalization; uses every opportunity to reinforce these techniques
Orchestrating an intense scene: therapist focuses on covering the physical/ medical as well as psychological symptoms of eating disorders. Therapists should discuss morbidity and mortality, comorbidities and long-term outcomes.	1 = Techniques are harsh and aggressive, passive, or divisive; or therapist undermines his/her words with neutral or soothing behaviors
	2 = May passively mention concerns ("This is a very serious illness") without tying this back to the patient, the session, the focus of treatment
	3 = Brief, general statements; medical *or* psychological symptoms and concerns
	4 = Provides information on medical and psychological sequela of eating disorders/outcomes (or detailed information on one but not the other) but not using personal or specific information
	5 = Some use of more personal elements in orchestrating an intense scene; family experience gathered in history is reflected in information discussed when orchestrating an intense scene
	6 =
	7 = Therapist covers medical and psychological concerns in a context that is meaningful and specific to family; ties these to the need for immediate treatment and action; takes advantage of opportunities to express concern and need for urgent action
Reducing guilt and blame: therapist should adopt a nonjudgmental stance, steer clear of blame and reshape both self and other blame in parents. Efforts by the patient to blame parents are skillfully reframed by the therapist.	1 = Therapist joins in blame or chastises parents ("Well, we all make mistakes"); judgmental and/or harsh attempts to diminish guilt/blame
	2 = Therapist misses or ignores opportunities to shape or challenge behaviors of guilt and blame in the family
	3 = Therapist responds to statements of guilt/blame with general statements rather than actively alleviating parental anxiety
	4 = Therapist takes advantage of most opportunities to reduce guilt or blame; works to shape the majority of instances of judgment or behaviors that impair parental empowerment
	5 = Includes more parental strengths or statements toward empowerment ("You can do this" or "You have the skills"); directs the family toward the ways they have managed problems effectively before

Rating codes	Examples and illustrations*

	6 = Greater warmth and strength-based assessments of parents; actively using opportunities to shape guilt and blame; continued direction toward previous success in problem solving, leveraging skills/knowledge of the family
	7 = Therapist takes advantage of virtually all opportunities to shape guilt and blame; works actively to empower parents; provides reassurance based on their own language, strengths and experiences; identifies their examples
Therapist agnostic to cause of AN: therapists should not introduce causality and should work to both neutralize causal statements and bring the focus back to current symptom focus; it is okay to discuss behaviors ("People with AN tend to be hard workers and often can be perfectionistic") but making personality statements ("People with AN are perfectionists") is not agnostic.	1 =
	2 = General statements such as "Those behaviors do not necessarily cause AN"; passive statements or failure to work to keep a current symptom focus
	3 = May identify personality traits ("People with anorexia are perfectionists") or make other statements of cause with withdrawal or attempts to neutralize that ("We know this disorder is genetic, but we don't know what actually causes it")
	4 = Makes noncausal statements *or* redirects to the current symptom focus; "Many people diet, but few get AN"; if causal statements are presented, efforts are made to address them by returning to a symptom focus
	5 = Increased frequency of opportunities to demonstrate agnosticism or reshape conversations around causality ("We do not know what causes eating disorders but we do know that parents do not")
	6 = Includes preemptive noncausal statements as well as previous elements
	7 = Statements stating that specific cause is not known, *and* present symptom focus; takes every opportunity to move away from causality; direct statements: "We do not know the specific cause of AN, like most cancers, but that does not keep us from focusing on treating the illness, as we will do in this treatment"
Modification of criticism: this is coded only in response to criticism (if none, mark N/A); criticism can be reframed, restated or externalized; does not include criticism from patient to parents or siblings, only from parents/siblings toward patient; note that in Session 1 the therapist may elicit comments ("How has AN changed your child's personality?") that may sound critical, but should not be rated as	1 = Responds to critical statements with general statements after a lapse from the delivery; harsh or judgmental response to criticism ("That sort of criticism won't help your daughter"); does not directly respond to critical comments but uses externalization at some point in the session
	2 = General comments without follow-up ("What do you think your daughter feels when she hears that?" without helping reshape or reframe the language/comment)
	3 =
	4 = Modifies many statements as they arise; does so in a relatively timely manner and with some skill
	5 = Greater fluency (speed and/or skill) of reframing/restating critical statements; uses externalization or other techniques to emphasis the divide between patient and AN

(Continued)

Rating codes	Examples and illustrations[*]
such unless the therapist fails to externalize the illness effectively in the session.	6 = 7 = Modifies virtually all critical statements quickly and immediately; may also include setting a groundwork for communication in session; skillful modification of criticism (nonjudgmental); delivers with this warmth and respect; critical statements are directly shaped with more appropriate language; critical examples are then brought back to externalization to help reinforce that this is the illness
Charging with refeeding: for Session 1 this is largely focused on charging the family with the family meal in Session 2; should *not* include assistance with renourishment/nutrition in this session.	1 = Solicits or encourages input from patient; provides specific description of a meal(s) 2 = Focuses on bringing food without indicating this is a meal (not a snack) or without stressing that this is a family meal; no specific challenge to provide a meal for increasing weight; does not encourage parents to work together 3 = References to parents in charge of renourishment with some, but not all, issues required to score at 4 4 = Injunction to bring a meal should be targeted at parents/caregivers *and* aligning caregivers if more than one present *and* focus of meal on weight gain/renourishment/return to health ("I want the two of you to bring a meal that you feel your starving daughter needs to eat to recover") 5 = Specific injunction around family meal that is not explanatory; additional statements regarding parental role as in charge of renourishment *or* parental empowerment/knowledge in renourishment ("You can do this," "You know how to feed your child and you need to begin to do that now to help her recover") 6 = 7 = Specific injunction around family meal that is not explanatory; parental empowerment/knowledge *and* parents being in charge throughout session ("You are an expert in your child and you know what he/she has needed to thrive until this terrible illness took over. This therapy helps parents learn how to renourish their children as you are going to do with your child. It will be challenging but I am confident you will meet that challenge.") *and* includes a statement about keeping the adolescent's healthy behaviors or independence intact

[*]Taken from:

Fitzpatrick, K. K., Accurso, E. C., Aspen, V., Forsberg, S. E., Le Grange, D., & Lock, J. (2015). Conceptualizing fidelity in FBT as the field moves forward: How we know when we're doing it right? In K. L. Loeb, D. Le Grange, & J. Lock (Eds.), *Family Therapy for Adolescent Eating and Weight Disorders: New Applications* (pp. 418–439).

Forsberg, S., Fitzpatrick, K. K., Darcy, A., Aspen, V., Accurso, E. C., Bryson, S. W., . . . Lock, J. (2015). Development and evaluation of a treatment fidelity instrument for family-based treatment of adolescent anorexia nervosa. *International Journal of Eating Disorders, 48*(1), 91–99.

Appendix VI: Fidelity Coding Framework: Session 2

Rating codes	*Examples and illustrations**
Providing feedback to the family regarding weight: the goal is to share weight with the family in a way that directs the session and lets them know that this is the framework by which we will assess between-session progress.	1 = Therapist response is in direct contrast to the weight (a concerned, heavily problem-oriented response to an appropriate increased weight, which should be met with congratulations, or a cheerful, chatty response to weight loss); *or* weight is taken and not shared
	2 = Shares information vaguely about weight ("She was up a bit") *or* negates/minimizes the importance of this weight ("I wouldn't worry too much") *or* provides information that normalizes lack of progress
	3 = Provides feedback near the beginning of the session; some specificity in sharing the weight; does not provide context
	4 = Provides feedback at the start of the session specific to weight; can be given in general terms but needs to provide direction for the session ("Her weight is down" or "Her weight is 89 pounds"); provides some context for the weight ("We will do this at the start of each session")
	5 = Provides feedback at the start of the session; more specificity in weight ("up two pounds from X to Y"), including graphing weight or writing down the numbers to share with the family; informs family that this will occur at each session and will be shared with the family
	6 = All of the elements of a "5" response and provides a general guideline for understanding or interpreting weight ("She is up half a pound which is good, but we need to work to increase that" or "Four pounds in one week is a bit concerning; it seems too much"); therapist delivers the weight with affect congruent to the degree of weight gain/loss
	7 = Provides feedback at the start of the session, providing both verbal and graphical representation of the change; explaining to parents the purpose of the weigh-in and the way this information will be used; discouraging weigh-ins outside of session; provides education about the purpose of the weigh-in (to provide exposure to weight for patient; to allow for assessment of progress toward goals, to activate AN in the session); provides specifics regarding expected weight progress (2 pounds a week)
Take a history of the family patterns around food prep, serving and discussion around eating: the goal is to understand the typical family structure around meal times, such that the therapist has a better idea of where	1 = The therapist passively observes a meal being served, may ask what items are, but does not engage in a discussion beyond this
	2 = Inquires about who chose the meal *or* encouragement to parents to serve *or* communication between parents on meal selection
	3 =
	4 = Most of the session is focused on the current meal, rather than a history of understanding what a family does at home; the therapist asks about the meal provided in the session

(Continued)

Rating codes	Examples and illustrations*
there may be AN-maintaining behaviors that can be focused on in session.	(meal content), gathers an understanding of how the meal was selected, and observes and questions around plating and serving of the session meal *or* the opposite (focus almost exclusively on similarity to home meal, rather than the current meal) 5 = Greater generalization to family meal at home *or* more skillful efforts at history gathering around the current meal; shopping, meal planning is reviewed (either for current meal or home meals—if *both*, then that is more of a 6) 6 = Gathers all of the foregoing and a good view of a daily or weekly menu (e.g., what did/do you serve for breakfast/lunch/dinner and snacks?). 7 = Therapist gathers specific information on the current meal (who chose the meal, did parents discuss between them, how did they choose, what did they choose) *and* how who served/chose/prepared this meal is similar to what happens in the family home *and* therapist makes attempts to gather this information from everyone in the family
Assist the family in understanding nutritional needs of the patient.	1 = Therapist encourages parents to "work it out for themselves" without assisting in how to do this; does not shape or assist family with understanding increased caloric needs associated with AN 2 = Reminding parents that "they know how" to feed their child without assisting them in working out what appropriate meals are like *or* may caution parents to stay away from certain foods ("You wouldn't want to introduce french fries, for example"); in this case, the therapist puts the idea out to the family that they should think about nutrition but does not provide any guidance on doing so; if a meal plan is being followed and is inadequate, the family is not instructed to increase nourishment 3 = May provide information on intake without bringing back to the current meal (or vice versa) *or* may refer the family to a meal plan or encourage them in following a strict meal plan provided by an outside source (rather than parental empowerment) 4 = Discussion of the need for more calories for weight restoration; some version of guidance ("Your child might need to eat as much as you and your husband, combined" or "The way your teenage son eats? That might be how much it takes to help your daughter gain weight") *and* some guidance based on the current meal (e.g., "Do you feel this is enough to help her gain weight?" or "The current meal does not seem sufficient to me to help her make progress"); basics here include helping parents think about frequency, size and caloric density of meals as a general minimum

Rating codes	Examples and illustrations*
	5 = More active attempts to help understand expected growth, caloric needs or progress ("Generally 500 calories a day extra will lead to one-half to one pound of weight gain per week. Where in your current routine do you think you could find that?"); may include specifics such as eliminating diet foods, identifying high-calorie density foods ("Changing from nonfat to regular milk can help you find about 200 more calories per day in your child's diet")
	6 =
	7 = The therapist provides specifics on nutrition: emphasis on fats, proteins, general calories; discussion of frequency, portioning *and* caloric density of foods to assist with weight gain; encourages away from empty or low calorie foods; uses the current meal to shape parental expectations or reinforce the appropriateness of the current meal
Align parents in efforts to work together in renourishing their child. (Note: if only one parent, but other adults involved, this can be coded for aligning adults involved in renourishment efforts).	1 = Therapist focuses on one parent or allows one person to "take over" renourishment efforts; failure to recruit both adults (if two are present); therapist negotiates directly with the patient in renourishment or allows parents to do so without shaping this behavior *or* sets parents against one another
	2 = Discuss areas of difference between parents without encouraging them to work this out between them or helping them problem-solve these differences; may allow some negotiation with patient for meal without shaping this back to parental efforts
	3 =
	4 = Therapist works to make certain both parents agree on the amount served to the patient during the in-session meal and notes that this is the same pattern that they should engage in at home, without specifically generalizing this to home behavior; may emphasize one area (e.g., type/amount/frequency) at the expense of others, but the message is clear that parents need to work together
	5 = May include assistance in identifying previously favored/current feared foods that may be important for renourishment with both parents agreeing upon these foods and/or plans for their reintroduction; therapist works with parents to insure that they agree on these aspects at most points or refers them back to working together on these issues (problem-solving techniques are generalized and reinforced for planning at home)
	6 = Parents are aligned in both their knowledge and efforts at specific changes; therapist points out when parents are on the same page and provides support for this; consistent messages of empowerment and alignment both within and outside of session

(Continued)

Rating codes	Examples and illustrations*
	7 = Continuous use of "the two of you" language or attempts to align parents when they appear separated in goals and implementation; repeated attempts to get both parents to discuss with one another/communicate regarding types/amounts/frequency of meals as well as how they have managed more difficult behaviors *and* these occur both in relation to the current meal and how they will do this outside of sessions (problem solving); focus on alignment in understanding the disease as a whole in addition to specific components (the problem of AN as well as the problem of "lunch")
One more mouthful: the goal is to help the parents engage AN and achieve a measure of success in helping their child do more than expected by AN. Therapists should be very active here, helping, guiding and even moving people about in session to maximize the likelihood for success. This is not coded on whether the patient takes a bite, but on the therapist's activity in helping the family engage AN toward this goal.	1 = Therapist allows family to eat what is brought/served without any assistance in adding more or engaging in a challenge with AN; may encourage the family to "work it out" without providing any strategies or feedback; therapist may not address the meal at all or engage parents in working on intake)
	2 = Therapist may make suggestions but is generally passive; allow for challenges to patient without empathy ("Just eat it and we can go home" is not shaped); therapist may ask about the meal being served without identifying or shaping amounts/types of food served; if patient eats compliantly, no efforts to introduce paradoxical injunction or amplify challenging aspects of the meal
	3 =
	4 = The therapist helps the parents with efforts toward shaping eating behaviors (verbal or behavioral) by keeping them focused on eating behaviors and engaging in different behaviors to increase compliance with these demands; provides support for appropriate/helpful eating behaviors and reshapes behaviors that limit renourishment efforts; paradoxical injunction if patient eating well but may not amplify this if continued compliance is present; empathy toward patient
	5 = Therapist actively supports parents, guides their behavior and is continuous in efforts to exhort them to manage AN behaviors; guides siblings away from this role if they attempt to take over/provides reminders that the siblings should not be in this role; challenges AN if little resistance is shown or encourages parents to amplify AN behaviors if they are minimally present; may provide a specific suggestion for increased intake if parents are unable to identify appropriate choices
	6 =
	7 = Therapist actively encourages the family to work to support the patient in eating more; provides encouragement for verbal strategies ("You need to eat this") as well as behavioral strategies (e.g., sitting next to patient); problem-solves with the family when facing resistance *or* provides a paradoxical injunction if patient is

Rating codes	Examples and illustrations*
	eating well (including making comments that may make eating more challenging, such as "That is an excellent meal filled with healthy fats; the cheese in particular makes that a more calorie-dense food") *or* increases food and intake until a challenging meal is presented to the patient; statements of warmth and empathy toward patient are encouraged ("We know this is hard for you" or "This is difficult but we are going to help you through it")
Setting parents on their way to work out among themselves how to renourish their child: efforts to support and empower parents, helping place the emphasis on parents as "in charge" of renourishment both in the session and in the interval between sessions.	1 = Therapist provides little direction toward renourishment, statements are limited to "I trust that you know what to do," "Go with your gut" or similar statements
	2 =
	3 = May provide a suggestion with greater direction ("Have you thought about how you will handle school lunches?" or "She needs more and that is something you can help her with by taking control")
	4 = Therapist squarely places responsibility for increased intake on parents; emphasizes the need for parental efforts at renourishment based on the patient's dire health and/or regressed ability to manage nourishment on his/her own; returns to parental strengths and knowledge as platforms for emphasizing intake ("If she was struggling as a child, you would have been able to help her take her medicine; you need to do that again, now")
	5 = Provides greater encouragement for thinking through specific challenges and may provide examples from other families when parents are stymied; helps identify challenges that parents may not be aware of/thinking about
	6 =
	7 = Repeated efforts supporting parental empowerment; therapist frames the problem of renourishment and provides specific prompts for parents ("What do you think you will do differently at breakfast? Snack? Lunch? Snack?"); identifies common challenges for parents (e.g., meals outside the home) and encourages discussion on how this problem will be solved; "developing a plan" with the family to address renourishment; therapist active and responsive in providing psychoeducation regarding intake and nutritional needs/impact of exercise and activity
Modifying parental and sibling criticism: this is as it sounds; fidelity depends on the speed and skill of shaping criticism—to be most effective critical comments should be shaped quickly.	1 = Responds to critical statements with general statements after a lapse from the delivery; harsh or judgmental response to criticism ("That sort of criticism won't help your daughter")
	2 = General comments without follow-up ("What do you think your daughter feels when she hears that" without helping reshape or reframe the language/comment)
	3 = General externalization ("That's AN") without reshaping, reframing or assisting the family in developing a more adaptive communication pattern

(Continued)

Rating codes	Examples and illustrations*
	4 = Modifies many statements as they arise; does so in a relatively timely manner and with some skill; uses externalization, reshaping, reframing critical statements (more than just externalization)
	5 = Greater fluency (speed and/or skill) in reframing/restating critical statements; uses externalization or other techniques to emphasis the divide between patient and AN
	6 = Generalizes importance of a supportive, nonjudgmental stance—directly addresses the role of critical communication in disrupting renourishment (uses statements made in therapy to generalize to more appropriate communication styles)
	7 = Modifies virtually all critical statements quickly and immediately; may also include setting a groundwork for communication in session; skillful modification of criticism (nonjudgmental); delivers this with warmth and respect; critical statements are directly shaped with more appropriate language; critical examples are then brought back to externalization to help reinforce that this is the illness
Externalization of illness	1 = Passive therapist; failure to respond to most opportunities to shape or reinforce externalization; does not use externalizing language or consistently uses externalizing language in an inappropriate way
	2 = May use externalizing statements in a vague or general manner ("That's AN") but not consistently or does not shape the language of others or tie to specific behaviors ("We can assume that conflict at home is driven by AN").
	3 =
	4 = Therapist uses externalizing language throughout; takes most opportunities to shape the language of the family or provides context to help understand behaviors as AN; may provide examples of the ways AN is active at mealtimes or use meal-centered activities ("This resistance to higher-calorie foods is what we see in AN"); includes use of externalization to shape criticism
	5 = Greater use of opportunities to help the family externalize; more active therapist; provides specific behaviors either brought up by family or observed in session to assist the family in externalization
	6 = Greater use of doing so in a way that reflects the family's language or experiences; helps the family recognize the importance of externalization in renourishment efforts; misses almost no opportunities to shape or reinforce externalization
	7 = Therapist uses the family's language and issues to reshape or reinforce externalization; uses every opportunity to reinforce these techniques; directly shapes criticism (where present) with externalization

Rating codes	Examples and illustrations*
Align patient with siblings for support: this involves finding ways for siblings to support the patient in managing difficult emotions, support them outside of session (by reducing negative emotions and preferably by increasing positive emotions) as well as directly coaching siblings to avoid renourishment.	1 = Allows or encourages sibling involvement in renourishment; spends time discussing conflict but not ways to reduce this if present in the sibling relationship 2 = 3 = 4 = Therapist attempts to get siblings to comfort patient or suggests that their role is to remain neutral to renourishment efforts and provide support after meals, without providing direct instruction; may support efforts made by the siblings in session with verbal praise and encouragement 5 = 6 = Some assistance with solving problems related to interactions (e.g., "They do not know how to get along"); proactive or direct instruction away from involvement in renourishment; support for statements that are encouraging *or* provides psychoeducation to continue to assist siblings in supporting patient 7 = Therapist addresses sibling concerns as well as patient concerns; provides examples of appropriate support *and* inappropriate support (e.g., renourishment efforts); assists in identifying specific areas the sibling(s) can be of assistance ("What did you used to do together?" or "How do you think you can comfort your sister/brother right now?"); assists with challenges in this area *or* support efforts made in session
Keep focus on AN and eating disorder behavior.	1 = Multiple topics discussed; focus on comorbidity; less than 50% of the session focused on eating disordered behavior; therapist allows for topics of discussion other than shape and weight concerns or reviews other topics, such as comorbidity; may lead the family to topics other than eating concerns even when that is a concern of the family 2 = 3 = Family concerns outside eating and weight concerns dominate the session; family distracted from or not engaged in the actual meal being eaten; therapist struggles to maintain focus and session has a disconnected or dysfluent feel to it; therapist hears a concern and provides specific feedback but does not help direct the family direct that toward the current meal 4 = Majority (75%) of this session spent discussing food/eating/shape/weight either directly in relation to the family meal or more generally; attempts to bring up other concerns are gently shaped back to the current session; brings focus to the current meal and elements of similarities and differences about this meal and typical meals at home 5 = Same as earlier, but also amplifies AN if this is not a concern ("easy eaters"); helps parents make the current meal a bit more like a meal at home

(Continued)

Rating codes	Examples and illustrations*
	6 = Holds greater focus on ED behaviors (85% or more of the session); largely focused on the current meal and assisting the family in understanding specific behaviors of AN—moving from general understanding of AN to a family-specific understanding of AN in their child
	7 = Therapist holds a strong focus on the meal/eating disorder behaviors; prompts the family through the goals of the session; manages attempts to bring up other topics with skills, speed and a return to eating disordered behavior as the focus; session focuses on parental concerns around AN and focus is maintained here
Agnosticism: therapists should not introduce causality and should work to both neutralize causal statements and bring the focus back to current symptom focus; it is okay to discuss behaviors ("People with AN tend to be hard workers and often can be perfectionistic") but making personality statements ("People with AN are perfectionists") is not agnostic.	1 =
	2 = General statements such as "Those behaviors do not necessarily cause AN"; passive statements or failure to work to keep a current symptom focus; discussion of comorbidity or other features with undue emphasis
	3 = May identify personality traits ("People with anorexia are perfectionists") or make other statements of cause with withdrawal or attempts to neutralize that ("We know this disorder is genetic, but we don't know what actually causes it")
	4 = Makes noncausal statements *or* redirects to the current symptom focus; "Many people diet, but few get AN"
	5 = Increased frequency of opportunities to demonstrate agnosticism or reshape conversations around causality; can acknowledge potential for comorbidity but return to the importance of current focus on AN ("Nothing trumps AN other than acute suicidality")
	6 =
	7 = Present symptom focus; takes every opportunity to move away from causality; direct statements ("We do not know the specific cause of AN, like most cancers, but that does not keep us from focusing on treating the illness, as we will do in this treatment")

*Taken from:
Fitzpatrick, K. K., Accurso, E. C., Aspen, V., Forsberg, S. E., Le Grange, D., & Lock, J. (2015). Conceptualizing fidelity in FBT as the field moves forward: How we know when we're doing it right? In K. L. Loeb, D. Le Grange, & J. Lock (Eds.), *Family Therapy for Adolescent Eating and Weight Disorders: New Applications* (pp. 418–439).
Forsberg, S., Fitzpatrick, K. K., Darcy, A., Aspen, V., Accurso, E. C., Bryson, S. W., . . . Lock, J. (2015). Development and evaluation of a treatment fidelity instrument for family-based treatment of adolescent anorexia nervosa. *International Journal of Eating Disorders, 48*(1), 91–99.

Appendix VII: Fidelity Coding Framework: Session 3 and Remainder of Phase I

Rating codes	Examples and illustrations*
Providing feedback to the family regarding weight: the goal is to share weight with the family in a way that directs the session and letting them know that this is the framework by which we will assess between-session progress.	1 = Therapist response is in direct contrast to the weight (a concerned, heavily problem-oriented response to an appropriate increased weight, which should be met with congratulations, or a cheerful, chatty response to weight loss); *or* weight is taken and not shared 2 = Shares information vaguely about weight ("She was up a bit") *or* negates/minimizes the importance of this weight ("I wouldn't worry too much") *or* provides information that normalizes lack of progress 3 = Provides feedback near the beginning of the session; some specificity in sharing the weight; does *not* provide context (e.g., no specific weight or how much up or down) 4 = Provides feedback at the start of the session specific to weight; can be given in general terms but needs to provide direction for the session ("Her weight is down" or "Her weight is 89 pounds"); provides some context for the weight ("We will do this at the start of each session"); affect and delivery of this are appropriate to the weight (e.g., if weight is down, tone is appropriately somber; with weight gain tone can be more encouraging and light) 5 = Provides feedback at the start of the session; more specificity in weight ("up two pounds from X to Y"), including graphing weight or writing down the numbers to share with the family; informs family that this will occur at each session and will be shared with the family 6 = All of the elements of a "5" response and provides a general guideline for understanding or interpreting weight ("She is up half a pound, which is good, but we need to work to increase that" or "Four pounds in one week is a bit concerning; it seems too much"); therapist delivers the weight with affect congruent to the degree of weight gain/loss; *and/or* shares the trajectory of weight ("You were 98, then lost half a pound, but this week you gained it back plus another pound, so you are up 1.5 pounds from when we started") 7 = Provides feedback at the start of the session, providing both verbal and graphical representation of the change; explaining to parents the purpose of the weigh-in and the way this information will be used; discouraging weigh-ins outside of session; provides education about the purpose of the weigh-in (to provide exposure to weight for patient; to allow for assessment of progress toward goals, to activate AN in the session); provides specifics regarding expected weight progress (2 pounds a week)

(Continued)

(Continued)

Rating codes	Examples and illustrations*
Did the therapist direct, redirect and focus therapeutic discussion on food and eating behaviors and their management until food, eating and weight behaviors and concerns were relieved? Focus on eating disorder behavior; if problem solving occurs and plan is set, the family and therapist may discuss other concerns.	1 = Therapist allows for topics of discussion other than shape and weight concerns or reviews other topics, such as comorbidity; may lead the family to topics other than eating concerns even when that is a concern of the family 2 = 50% or less of session focused on eating and weight concerns 3 = Family concerns outside eating and weight concerns dominate the session; therapist struggles to maintain focus and session has a disconnected or dysfluent feel to it; therapist hears a concern and provides specific feedback but does not help direct the family ("She eats the same foods all the time; she has always been like that"; Tx: "That's control" *instead of* "That kind of flexibility is hard to develop and is something you need to keep your mind on—as we are talking about what breakfast looks like, I wonder if there are foods you would like to see her add in") 4 = 75% of session is focused on eating disorder concerns and challenges; the therapist "keeps an eye on the ball" of returning to the discussion of food, eating, shape and weight concerns even when parents may be distracted by other content; therapist may interrupt or redirect focus when necessary to prevent moving off topic; review of meals during the past week 5 = Continual efforts to make connections to eating, shape and weight concerns; fluidity in returning to these concerns (the session feels like it builds momentum); return to history to avoid arguments ("She used to like eggs, so what you are hearing now"), in addition to review of meals from past week, work toward future problem solving; see example at #3 for a good example of this 6 = 85% or more of the session focused on eating disorder concerns; uses history, esp. from Session 2, to keep focus on meals (specific and concise focus); also uses a forward focus momentum *if current* concerns are managed (e.g., "What will you serve at breakfast tomorrow? What about summer coming up, how will that change/how can you stay on track?"); greater framework for moving from specific to general problem solving. 7 = Skillful use of redirection; efforts to leverage the family's own concerns (esp. as described in previous sessions) to keep the focus on eating disorder behaviors; reminds parents of the importance of this focus; encourages this focus outside of session as well (generalization—see code earlier)
Did the therapist discuss, support and help parental dyad's efforts at refeeding? Note: this code is primarily	1 = Therapist may place focus on exhorting patient to be involved in eating or encourages compliance, rather than focusing parents on overcoming resistance; fails to assist family in their understanding of needs around renourishment

Rating codes	Examples and illustrations*
alignment but also on parental control; if there is a single parent, you can still code here, but focus would be on empowerment rather than alignment. Nutrition advice and understanding caloric needs also fit here.	2 = May note that current diet is insufficient (or sufficient) but fails to follow up with family regarding adequacy of current nutrition; may focus on debate with patient to increase intake; may attempt to bolster the healthy part of the patient in a way that ends in debate or upset (Tx: "You seem like the kind of girl who . . ."; Patient: "You don't know me!")
	3 = Focus largely on parents, but may include patient or siblings; fails to redirect efforts by siblings to be involved in renourishment or mistakenly encourages one parent to be in charge (rather than supportive of each other even if one manages more meals than the other); may help think about frequency, size, caloric density *or* exercise, but fails to address some domains that are raised as problematic
	4 = Focus of efforts on parental alignment and communication; places emphasis on parental control over renourishment and working out problems between parents; evaluation of efforts in terms of increasing intake, decreasing exercise and/or overcoming general resistance; addresses (or attempts to) the different areas identified by the family as problematic for renourishment; if patient is eating well, the therapist engages with the healthy part of the patient; provides some examples, if necessary or acknowledges parent strength in avoiding divisive behaviors ("AN often finds the small fissures in our relationships and magnifies them; that's why your husband just doesn't know how to make eggs anymore ☺"); helps focus the family on the topic of renourishment (see prompt at #3)
	5 = Alignment may extend beyond eating to other behaviors; ties together challenges and keeps family focused on issues until these are resolved; good use of parental problem-solving skills to develop a plan for renourishment; if required, assistance in understanding nutrition goals; may engage with healthy part of patient to direct treatment (e.g., Patient: "Having scales in the house is really difficult for me"; Thx: "Sounds like that is a change you would like to make. Parents, what do you think about this?"); uses opportunities in session to align parents even when they sound like disagreements ("It sounds like you both want the same thing—you'd like your daughter to eat more, but maybe you are getting sidetracked by the details of what that is. I feel like you might be in violent agreement here!")
	6 = All of the foregoing and assistance in modeling or teaching skills to keep parents supported (e.g., selective ignoring of AN behaviors); therapist identifies and restates challenges in terms of AN behaviors; therapist may

(Continued)

Rating codes	Examples and illustrations*
	assist parents in identifying future challenges; focuses on renourishment efforts, including management of intake, exercise, flexibility of foods chosen; good problem-solving focus for parents, allows them space to come up with suggestions and supports what they want to implement *or* draws outside concerns back to renourishment framework ("You are right, going back to school is tough for many reasons . . . how do you think you will tackle the most important focus of helping her eat while at school?")
	7 = Focus on strengths as well as challenges (strength-based focus); appropriate reminders about the role of siblings if they are involved (this is different than ahead, which is ways siblings can help); both specific advice and generalized to home environment ("She used to like mashed potatoes, so that might be something I've heard as being part of what you will reintroduce. Are there other foods like that?")
Did the therapist discuss, support and help family to evaluate efforts of siblings to help their affected sibling?	1 = Therapist encourages sibling's efforts at renourishment, outlines divisive relationships between siblings or holds one up against the other in terms of health; fails to intervene in any significant negative interactions
	2 =
	3 = Therapist notes the importance of sibling relationships without pointing out supportive aspects of the relationship ("Brothers and sisters are important in getting better")
	4 = Therapist addresses sibling relationship in a way designed to make this supportive; may ask what has been engaging previously, may ask sibling and/or parents (or even healthy part of patient, if possible) about activities that have been useful
	5 = Amplifies existing strengths (activities they have already done together), draws upon sibling experience with healthy part of patient to continue to help the family and patient distinguish from AN; provides skills and strengths for managing AN ("I know AN doesn't like it when you are around, but you have to remember what it has been like when you've been with your sister, before the disorder")
	6 =
	7 = Helps identify ways or builds upon things demonstrated in session that soothe patient (e.g., "What would you normally do to help her feel better? Could you do that?"); deliberate focus away from sibling as agent of renourishment; potential for identifying commonalities between patient and sibling or sibling as a model for adolescent development

Rating codes	Examples and illustrations*
Modification of criticism: this is coded only in response to criticism (if none, mark N/A); criticism can be reframed, restated or externalized; does not include criticism from patient to parents or siblings, only from parents/siblings toward patient.	1 = Responds to critical statements with general statements after a lapse from the delivery; harsh or judgmental response to criticism ("That sort of criticism won't help your daughter") 2 = General comments without follow-up ("What do you think your daughter feels when she hears that?" without helping reshape or reframe the language/comment) 3 = General externalization ("That's AN") without reshaping, reframing or assisting the family in developing more adaptive communication pattern 4 = Modifies many statements as they arise; does so in a relatively timely manner and with some skill; uses externalization, reshaping, reframing critical statements (more than just externalization) 5 = Greater fluency (speed and/or skill) in reframing/restating critical statements; uses externalization or other techniques to emphasize the divide between patient and AN 6 = Generalizes importance of a supportive, nonjudgmental stance—directly addresses the role of critical communication in disrupting renourishment (uses statements made in therapy to generalize to more appropriate communication styles) 7 = Modifies virtually all critical statements quickly and immediately; may also include setting a groundwork for communication in session; skillful modification of criticism (nonjudgmental); delivers this with warmth and respect; critical statements are directly shaped with more appropriate language; critical examples are then brought back to externalization to help reinforce that this is the illness
Did the therapist continue to distinguish adolescent patient and her/his interests from those of AN (externalize the illness): importantly, this focuses on externalization; efforts may be made to help the patient do so, but this code is primarily focused on assisting parents with separating the patient from AN.	1 = Passive therapist; failure to respond to most opportunities to shape or reinforce externalization 2 = May use externalizing statements in a vague or general manner 3 = Does not directly teach externalization but may use the language of externalization ("That is the illness"); may make general, brief statements but does not tie these to specific behaviors ("That's AN") 4 = Therapist reinforces this in session once or twice; if the patient is able to demonstrate healthy behaviors or statements, these are expanded upon; may use the family's language or experience *and/or* when opportunities arise, therapist identifies areas where parents are not externalizing and assists them in doing so more effectively (teaching externalization around specific behaviors) 5 = Greater use of opportunities to help the family externalize; more active therapist; identifies the patient's areas of strength and uses these to help amplify the ways in which AN has caused difficulties or hearkens back ("Remember when we said AN does X,Y, Z behaviors ... this is an example of that); provides continuity between sessions with externalizations

(*Continued*)

Rating codes	Examples and illustrations*
	6 = Greater use of doing so in a way that reflects the family's language or experiences; uses patient's experiences and struggles to highlight differences between AN and patient and encourages patient to make these changes as well, if possible
	7 = Therapist uses the family's language and issues to reshape or reinforce externalization; uses every opportunity to reinforce these techniques; uses opportunities to help patient and parents identify healthy vs. AN behaviors and support the former while externalizing the latter.
Therapist agnostic to cause of AN: therapists should not introduce causality and should work to both neutralize causal statements and bring the focus back to current symptom focus; it is okay to discuss behaviors ("People with AN tend to be hard workers and often can be perfectionistic") but making personality statements ("People with AN are perfectionists") is not agnostic.	1 =
	2 = General statements such as "Those behaviors do not necessarily cause AN"; passive statements or failure to work to keep a current symptom focus
	3 = May identify personality traits ("People with anorexia are perfectionists") or make other statements of cause with withdrawal or attempts to neutralize that ("We know this disorder is genetic, but we don't know what actually causes it")
	4 = Makes noncausal statements *or* redirects to the current symptom focus; "Many people diet, but few get AN"
	5 = Increased frequency of opportunities to demonstrate agnosticism or reshape conversations around causality
	6 =
	7 = Statements stating that specific cause is not known, *and* present symptom focus; takes every opportunity to move away from causality; direct statements ("We do not know the specific cause of AN, like most cancers, but that does not keep us from focusing on treating the illness, as we will do in this treatment")

*Notes:

These codes are examples and do not necessarily encompass all the possible scores at these different points. By the same token, behaviors that are keyed at a particular point but had elements of a more skillful or effective delivery can be scored higher (or lower if less effective).

Therapists may deliver mixed messages—in these cases, the rater must determine the extent to which the mixed message decreased the score. It should be noted that one 7 is not likely offset by 5 and 6 responses; however, a 5 and a 3 would likely also not equal a 4, as presenting a mixed message decreases fidelity in and of itself.

**Taken from:

Fitzpatrick, K. K., Accurso, E. C., Aspen, V., Forsberg, S. E., Le Grange, D., & Lock, J. (2015). Conceptualizing fidelity in FBT as the field moves forward: How we know when we're doing it right? In K. L. Loeb, D. Le Grange, & J. Lock (Eds.), *Family Therapy for Adolescent Eating and Weight Disorders: New Applications* (pp. 418–439).

Forsberg, S., Fitzpatrick, K. K., Darcy, A., Aspen, V., Accurso, E. C., Bryson, S. W., . . . Lock, J. (2015). Development and evaluation of a treatment fidelity instrument for family-based treatment of adolescent anorexia nervosa. *International Journal of Eating Disorders, 48*(1), 91–99.

Appendix VIII: Phase II Treatment Goals

	Example	Where/when are these present	Where/when are these absent	Treatment goals
Ongoing eating disorder behaviors	Secretive exercise (crunches, jumping jacks in room)	This is an ongoing compulsive behavior that increased in response to removal of participation in sports at initiation of treatment.	When playing soccer, the patient did not engage in these behaviors; however, soccer eventually became an opportunity to engage in compulsive exercise.	Return to healthy physical activity 1. Assess motivations for return to sport 2. Identify steps toward gradual return to sport while monitoring pathological exercise 3. Encourage parents to revisit strategies for increased monitoring of secretive exercise
Body image concerns	Patient engages in frequent body comparisons with friends (in person and on social media) and verbalizes distress about weight as compared to friends.	These behaviors intensify in the context of a peer group that engages in discussion about dieting and body shape/size.	Events precipitate body comparisons frequently throughout day. Screen-time is limited when patient is doing homework.	Decrease frequency/ impact of comparisons

Developmental strengths	Patient is able to verbalize consequences of comparisons and frustration regarding societal standards of beauty and recognizes this behavior as problematic to her recovery. Patient is social and has a diverse and supportive group of friends.
Developmental challenges	Patient relies on validation from peers, has low self-worth and has excessive self-standards leading to frequent perception of failure.
Parental strengths	Parents have balanced expectations for achievement and encourage patient to practice flexibility and spontaneity. Parents model effective communication.
Parental challenges	Parents have difficulty setting limits around typical adolescent behaviors and identifying consequences to problematic behaviors (e.g., frequent angry outbursts with parents and siblings during periods of heightened anxiety/stress).

Appendix IX: Phase III Readiness Assessment

Is the adolescent fully weight-restored?

1. If the adolescent is not fully weight-restored, what are the barriers? Is the adolescent actively engaged in working on the barriers and is he or she appropriately motivated in achieving full weight restoration?

2. Has the adolescent had sufficient practice with meeting the demands of independent eating?

3. Do the adolescent and family feel that goals related to independent eating have been accomplished? For example, does the family feel that there is a sense of normalcy around eating routines that reflect historical patterns or desired patterns they have identified in the process of treatment?

4. Is the adolescent back to most if not all typical activities (attending school regularly, spending time with peers, participating in activities of interest)? If not, is this because of ongoing concerns for the ED, or due to other areas of challenge that may be addressed in Phase III?

Appendix X: Phase III Treatment Planning Guide

Theme	Typical development	Common challenges	Therapeutic interventions
Body image concerns	Body changes occur with puberty in early stages of adolescent development. Certain body image ideals are integrated based on feedback from one's sociocultural environment.	There are concerns about attractiveness and overemphasis on body image in self-worth. Physical maturation is perceived as different than peers. Physical maturation is a marker of increased independence that is cause for discomfort.	Provide psychoeducation on components of a healthy body and self-image. Build areas of self-worth outside of body image. Problem-solve triggers that maintain negative body image (e.g., wearing a bathing suit). Encourage activities that broaden one's relationship with his/her body (e.g., focusing on health and utility rather than appearance). Address fears around emerging sexuality, increased responsibility and pressures and identify strategies to increase a sense of safety.
Communication	Independent voice is developing—teens begin to separate their views from those of their family and begin to consider alternative perspectives and practice communication of these with family and peers. Negotiation skills are learned and perspective taking, cognitive flexibility and other abstract-thinking skills continue to develop as adolescence progresses.	Difficulty expressing views in the context of social concerns/ fear of judgment or making a social mistake. Conflict avoidance. Uncertainty in needs, wants and goals reflecting underlying emotion regulation challenges	Teach interpersonal effectiveness skills. Practice engaging family communication in areas of conflict with a focus on encouraging practice of basic communication skills (e.g., reflective listening, validation).

(Continued)

Theme	Typical development	Common challenges	Therapeutic interventions
Managing the spectrum of impulsivity to inhibition	Typically adolescents are not able to employ complex executive functioning skills given brain maturational processes. Impulsive actions are typical with failure to think through consequences.	High impulsivity resulting in risk taking behaviors in multiple domains vs. high levels of inhibition and averseness to risk leading to missed opportunities for growth and learning	Orient families to typical vs. atypical/problematic levels of risk taking tailored to specific behavioral concerns. Help families set contingencies around problem behaviors. When the problem is inhibition, encourage families to create a supportive framework for novel experiences that may challenge and expand adolescent confidence around spontaneity/uncertainty.
Difficulties in emotion regulation	Hormonal changes may intensify felt emotional experience. Adolescents may experience emotions as out of control or confusing and may have difficulty verbalizing emotions and using emotional data to effectively support decision making.	Maladaptive coping strategies to escape/avoid aversive emotional states, resulting in a cycle of emotion dysregulation and lost opportunities to learn new skills to regulate emotions. Patients and families may see emotions as problematic/to be avoided.	Provide basic education on role of emotions/model of emotion. Encourage families to reflect on their own beliefs and response to expressed emotion. Teach basic emotion regulation skills as needed.
Perfectionism/Low self-confidence	Adolescents seek feedback on their value/worth through peer comparisons; can be overly sensitive to punishment (mistakes), less so to rewards; may require assistance in incorporating these experiences into sense of self in a balanced and nonjudgmental fashion.	Unrealistically high standards may be reinforced through heightened attempts to succeed (overworking, hyperattention to detail and relying on objective measures of success). Consequence of perfectionistic ideals is fear of mistakes, avoidance or hypervigilance and unending quest for achievement that is unrelenting and unfulfilled.	Assist families in exploring consequences of perfectionistic beliefs and behaviors. Encourage exposure framework to support management of perfectionistic behaviors and testing perfectionistic beliefs.

Index

For Product Safety Concerns and Information please contact our EU
representative GPSR@taylorandfrancis.com
Taylor & Francis Verlag GmbH, Kaufingerstraße 24, 80331 München, Germany